Dr. J. Russell Turney

LEAVE A LEGACY

Increasing Missionary Longevity

FOREWORD
Dr. Greg Mundis

WIPF & STOCK · Eugene, Oregon

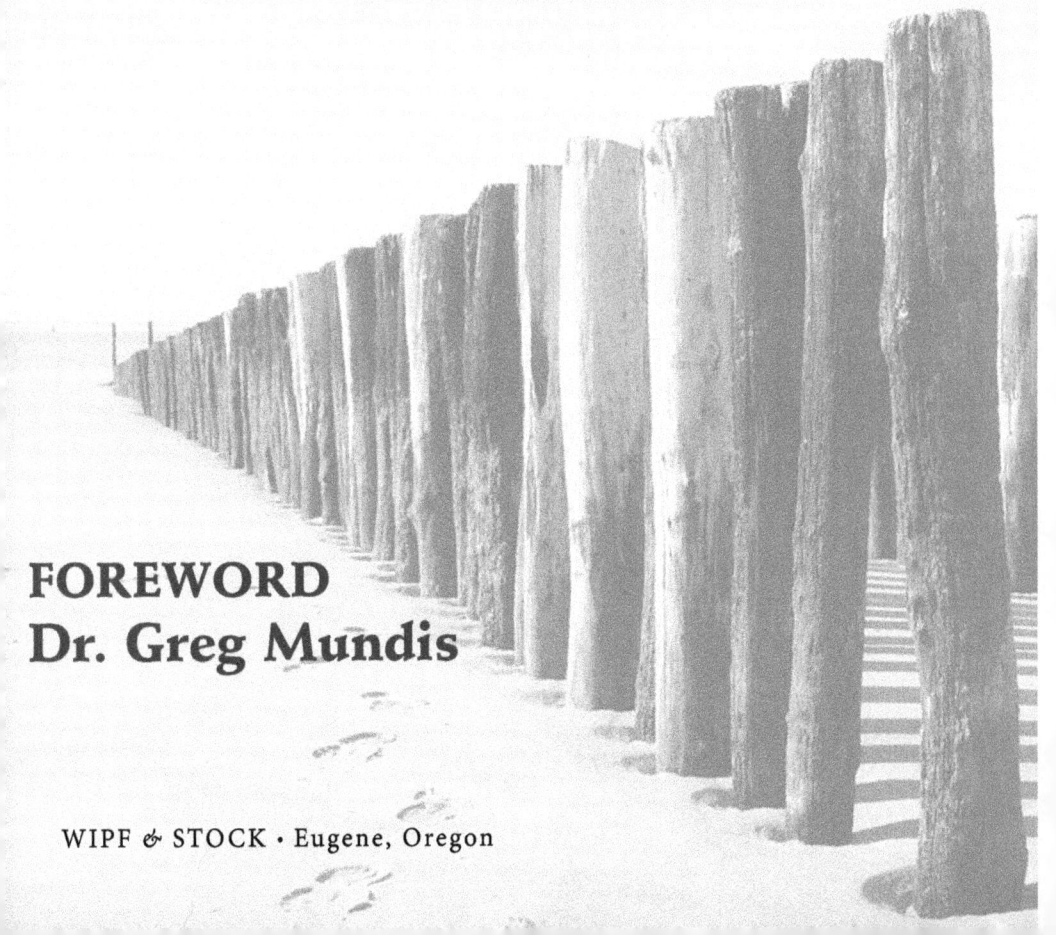

Wipf and Stock Publishers
199 W 8th Ave, Suite 3
Eugene, OR 97401

Leave a Legacy
Increasing Missionary Longevity
By Turney, J. Russell and Mundis, Greg
Copyright©2013 APTS Press
ISBN 13: 978-1-4982-9481-2
Publication date 12/15/2015
Previously published by APTS Press, 2013

This edition is published by Wipf and Stock
Publishers by arrangement with APTS Press.

FOREWORD

I am privileged to recommend this book by Russ Turney, who has wonderfully served the Assemblies of God over several decades. His experiences, expertise, and educational contribution are evidenced in this writing, and I know it will be a blessing to the body of Christ and particularly to the missionary family.

Russ recognizes from Scripture the conflicts that can develop among children of the Kingdom (i.e. believers) and offers sound advice for biblical resolution. He also offers modern educational methodologies and helps that are available to alleviate and resolve conflict, thus enabling missionaries to remain on the field for the long haul.

I highly recommend this for your reading and encourage you to implement its principles in your life and ministry.

Dr. Greg Mundis Executive Director
Assemblies of God World Missions (USA)

AUTHOR'S PREFACE

"Today we will hear from one of God's heroes who gave up everything to follow Him. . . ." Missionaries have heard this or similar statements repeatedly in church services when they return in the U.S., and many are uncomfortable with them. Often placed on a pedestal, those who serve in other countries know well their own humanity and need for daily surrender. As a youth more than fifty years ago, I had a deep respect and appreciation for those serving in distant lands. When missionaries came to our church sharing their vision and telling their stories, my own spiritual growth was challenged.

My appreciation for these special servants continued to grow as we interacted with missionaries during fifteen years of pastoral and youth ministry. Our family prayed for and supported them, and on several occasions traveled to the field to work with them in outreaches and church planting events. The two churches we were privileged to pastor encouraged missions, held mission conventions, and enthusiastically helped those who were living in other cultures in fulfillment of God's call on their lives.

Later, when God called us to Asia as missionaries with the Assemblies of God World Missions (AGWM), each member of our family faced his/her own challenges. We felt the impact of separation from loved ones, isolation, and occasional confusion. We encouraged our three children to see life and ministry as an adventure, and the unknown as an opportunity for the Lord to show us His greatness. They responded well and over the next ten years, as each left home to begin their own journey, we again faced all of the normal emotions of joy, anticipation, emptiness and loss, along with a recognition that God's miraculous hand was guiding our children as He had us in earlier years.

Now, after forty-five years of full time ministry with thirty of those in missions, my love and appreciation for my fellow missionaries has continued to increase immeasurably. I have seen those who finished their missionary careers with grace, joy, dignity, and with a clear sense of fulfillment. We have seen others because of health issues or situations beyond of their control, challenged to readjust their goals. Mixed in were a few who left missions for other difficult and heart breaking reasons bringing great stress to them and others around them.

The focus of this project emerged out of their struggles and our experiences. My initial desire was to research, identify, and evaluate the major reasons people who had been serving within the Asia Pacific Region left missions. This would include a twenty-year timeframe to help provide a cross section of people, time, and countries. Two things emerged from that research. The first was a realization that not all of the information I needed was available. The files did not provide the underlying, hidden reasons people resigned, which left gaps in the research. The second was a realization that the primary focus should not be on the past, but the future. How this material might help new candidates coming into missions emerged as a strategic goal. What lessons could be learned from past mistakes that would help new personnel adjust better, serve longer, and be more effective in missions? These questions helped shape the research and focus of this project. If reading this material helps clarify some of the issues that will be faced, if it strengthens the resolve to stay focused on Jesus' plan, if it perpetuates greater effectiveness in cross-cultural ministry, if it helps those at home to better support those who are on the field, then my goal will have been achieved.

J. Russell Turney
Asia Pacific Regional Director
AGWM - U.S.A.
Springfield MO
May 2013

TABLE OF CONTENTS

1 STATEMENT OF PROBLEM

The Apostle Paul provides one of the greatest examples of finishing well in missions. He summarized his life in 2 Timothy 4:7 where he writes, "I have fought the fight, I have finished the race, I have kept the faith."[1] He contrasts these words just three verses later by saying, "Demas, because he loved this world, has deserted me and gone to Thessalonica." Finishing well in missions is no easy task and requires significant effort by all who believe they are called by the Lord to serve cross-culturally in ministry. Finishing well was a challenge when the Church began nearly 2000 years ago, and it remains a challenge today.

The Problem Addressed by the Project

This project will address the problem of Asia Pacific (AP) missionaries leaving service early without finishing their missionary careers well. There are factors that negatively affect missionary longevity and increase attrition. There has never been a comprehensive study of AP regional missionaries that provides the reasons for missionary attrition or longevity. This research will identify issues that negatively affect missionary longevity and factors that positively help guard against attrition.

Factors Impacting Missionary Longevity

Within the Assemblies of God World Mission (AGWM), various factors impact the ability of personnel to remain at their place of service, and often it is believed that more could have been done to prevent them from leaving missions. Some say personnel leave due to an inability to make cultural adjustments, with culture shock impacting each member of the family differently. Unrealistic expectations can be a weight that hinders them. Occasionally, there is a lack of support either from those back home or on the field.

[1] All Scripture quotations, unless otherwise noted, are from New International Version (E. Brunswick, NJ: International Bible Society, 1984).

Character flaws that were not clearly seen earlier become more apparent after arriving on the mission field. There are some who are searching for God's will, and because they love missions they are not clear on the difference between that love and a clear call. Other factors that may affect longevity of service are language learning, conflicts on the field, or other unexpected or misunderstood circumstances that are often encountered.

During a twenty-year time frame (1986–2005), AGWM commissioned 2100 candidates for appointment. In 1985 there were 1394 total appointed missionaries, and at the end of 2005 there were 2045.[2] These numbers do not include associates who serve for one to two years. During that twenty-year time span, over 2100 candidates were commissioned, but the total number of missionaries grew by less than 700. Losses due to retirement, death, or withdrawals for health reasons are unavoidable and understood. However, often missionaries leave for reasons that are less acceptable and are even hurtful to themselves and others.

Missionaries who leave without completing their assignment affect not only the country where they worked and the mission-sending agency, but they also cause consternation in the minds of sending churches. The sending churches question why missionaries succumb to the pressure of working cross-culturally and leave just when they are at the point of making a contribution to the work. Missionary attrition affects the entire missionary and church network that seeks to reach the world for Christ.

Purpose

The purpose of this project is to develop, apply and evaluate missionary learning processes within the AGWM U.S. Asia Pacific Region to assist personnel to avoid preventable attrition, overcome hindrances to longevity and finish their missionary careers well.

The purpose of this project is to describe the primary factors of avoidable missionary attrition within the Asia Pacific Region of AGWM U.S., with the goal of helping more personnel finish well in their missionary career.

Significance

This project is significant because its outcomes will impact Asia Pacific missionaries in the following ways:

1.   It will provide a comprehensive study of AGWM Asia Pacific missionaries that examines the full scope of missionary attrition and longevity.

----

[2] "AGWM Annual Growth Rate Statistics: Compiled for the Years1985–2005," (Springfield, Missouri: Personnel and Family Life Department, Assemblies of God World Missions, 2008, photocopied).

2. It will identify the attrition rates between different categories of missionaries. Some of the categories have been in place longer than others, and it is helpful to see if some have a greater attrition rate than others.
3. It will compare the attrition rate for each five-year time frame from 1985 to 2005 to assess whether the attrition rate has reduced or increased. This study will evaluate the available data to determine the attrition rate and better identify and address the factors that can cause attrition.
4. It will provide insight into the attrition rate of the different candidate age groups and single missionaries.
5. It will assess the difference that the screening process makes to missionary attrition or longevity.
6. It will provide insight gleaned from veteran missionaries into the factors important to missionary longevity and their ability to remain active in missions.
7. Information derived from this research will assist future mission personnel in serving longer and more effectively in cross cultural ministry.
8. Information gathered in the research phase of this project will assist the Asia Pacific Region's candidate orientation process to better equip the organization to prepare personnel.
9. As Asia Pacific Regional Director, this project is significant to me in my leadership role in AGWM. During my years of missionary service both on the field and in this leadership capacity, I have seen missionaries finish well and witnessed the struggles and pain of missionaries who have not successfully finished their course. This project will assist me in helping to close the attrition gap. It is my desire to enable all AP missionaries to finish well.

Research Questions

1. What spiritual/biblical factors contribute to missionary attrition or longevity of service?
2. What personal and relational factors contribute to missionary attrition or longevity of service?
3. What organizational factors contribute to the process of missionary formation that impact attrition or longevity?

Scope of Research

This project's scope:

1. Will include research within the Assemblies of God World Mission USA (AGWM) and no other mission organizations. Some general observations are made regarding approved candidates for the organization.
2. Will include countries and personnel found within the Asia Pacific Region of the AGWM. This will not include information from other regions of the world.
3. Will include research done by other mission organizations with some limited comparisons made. However, the application in this project is done within the Asia Pacific Region's missionary personnel.
4. The research is limited to a twenty-year time frame, from 1986-2005 because this includes at least one generation of missionaries.

Definitions

AGWM—Assemblies of God World Missions is the missionary sending agency that sends missionaries from the United States to other countries and cultures.

Asia Pacific Region—a specific region of the world defined by AGWM as twenty island nations within the Pacific and fourteen countries within east Asia— Mongolia, Japan, Korea, Taiwan, Vietnam, Cambodia, Laos, Thailand, Myanmar, Malaysia, Singapore, Indonesia, East Timor, and the Philippines. The total number of countries within the Asia Pacific Region is thirty-five when North Korea is included.

Attrition—defined as a loss of personnel from missions for any reason. Sending agencies do recognize that some attrition is for positive reasons and can have minimal negative impact on the field.

Missionary—a person who works cross-culturally among people groups and cultures for the purpose of sharing the gospel and reaching people for Christ. His or her full-time role is focused on evangelism, helping start churches, training national workers, or serving in a compassion ministry role.

Missionary Associate (MA)—this refers to those who work outside the U.S. on a one to two year assignment in a missions setting.

Special Assignment (SA)—this is a contractual category whereby a contract is signed for three to four years. This is considered an appointed mission category.

Appointed Special (AS)—a category whereby a person has a specialized ministry such as youth, children, construction, etc.

Appointed General (AG)—the most common category whereby a person is appointed with the broadest scope of ministry.

Specialized Service (SP)—a specific category that is designed to include those who come into missions from unusual circumstances (i.e., retired military chaplains, district leaders, etc.) who come into world missions for four or more years often after serving many years stateside.

Missionary Kid (MK)—a term used to identify children who have lived on the mission field with their parents.

God-given missionary call—an inner awareness that a person has been chosen to serve the Lord cross-culturally. This awareness comes from the Holy Spirit and is normally confirmed by others who recognize and affirm that call.

Retirement age—defined as the date and age when someone actually retires, and is not necessarily the retirement age as defined by the U.S. government.

Assumptions

I assume that:

1. Each person who is approved for missionary service by AGWM has met the basic requirements for mission appointment and successfully completed a screening process. This also indicates that he or she has a clear call to mission service and a commitment to live and work in a cross-cultural setting.

2. Missionary and administrative personnel of the Assemblies of God World Mission (AGWM) Asia Pacific region are Pentecostal, and that each person appointed has a clear understanding of the infilling of the Holy Spirit and has experienced his or her own personal Pentecost.

3. There are reasons people leave missionary service early and that these reasons are identifiable.

4. With proper attention, attrition can be reduced in the missionary force and longevity can be enhanced.

Methodology

This project is accomplished through a process involving:

1. A review of pertinent literature on missionary attrition, spiritual/biblical models of service longevity, and personal and organizational factors to identify issues crucial to missionary longevity.

2. An analysis of available personnel records from 1986 to 2005 to identify factors leading to missionary attrition.

3. The development and evaluation of a program to introduce and prepare new missionaries to cross-cultural ministry and to help them deal with issues leading to attrition.
4. The development and evaluation of a process of on-going training for veteran missionaries in order to help them deal with attrition issues and to introduce them to factors that will help them finish well.

Conclusion

This project evaluates significant factors contributing to missionary longevity within the Asia Pacific Region with the purpose of helping missionaries finish their missionary careers well. It addresses the research questions that address the spiritual/biblical, personal and relational, and organizational factors that contribute to missionary longevity. The research will involve information from numerous sources and geographic areas, however, the application is for orientation and training systems within the Asia Pacific Region to prepare new missionary candidates and equip veteran missionaries in how to deal with attrition issues that impact their ability to finish their missionary service well.

The result of this project is the development and implementation of a comprehensive program that focuses on preparing new and veteran missionaries to deal with issues that lead to attrition and help them understand factors crucial to their longevity of service to the Lord in cross-cultural ministry and finishing their careers well.

Examination of Factors Impacting Longevity on the Field

The next three chapters will examine pertinent literature on missionary attrition, longevity, and organizational models that affect missionary attrition, longevity, and the ability to finish well. This chapter will look at Personal Factors Affecting Missionary Longevity. The two chapters that follow will focus on Organizational Factors Impacting Missionary Longevity, and Biblical/Spiritual Factors Impacting Missionary Longevity

Examination of Factors Affecting Missionary Longevity

This section examines literature which highlight factors that directly impact missionary success and longevity. These factors include psychological factors, culture shock, unrealistic expectations, God's call to cross-cultural ministry, and generational factors. All of these influence missionary outcomes positively or negatively and have a direct causal effect on missionary attrition.

Reasons for Missionary Attrition

Missionary attrition is a sad reality in missions. It is crucial for my study that the reasons missionaries leave missions are identified. This section will examine literature in the field of missionary attrition to identify reasons for attrition.

Frank Allen, in *Why Do They Leave? Reflections on Attrition*, addresses missionary attrition in general and identifies personal and organizational reasons missionaries leave. He concludes that missionaries leave early because (1) they lack the necessary ministry gifts needed in the area they serve; (2) culture shock causes discouragement that leads to early departure; (3) missionary expectations are not in line with the realities on the field; (4) moral failure due to sexual immorality impacts married as well as single missionaries; (5) family problems because of overly permissive or overly strict parenting styles create conflicts within the home; (6) disagreements with the mission-sending agency results in conflict with field leaders; (7) conflicts with other missionaries because of the American penchant towards individualism, and (8) language acquisition difficulties.[1]

Information about missionary failure or attrition that is of comparative benefit for my research is Craig Storti's *The Art of Crossing Cultures* in which he lists statistical information about expatriate worker loss. Storti addresses attrition from a Western cultural perspective and highlights reasons why people leave early. Storti says missionary failure in all types of agencies takes a human, economic and political toll. He reveals that more than thirty-three percent of American missionaries leave early because they are not able to adapt to their new work or living environments.[2] Storti examines the attrition rate in the Peace Corps and found their overall attrition rate was a fairly constant ten to twenty percent. Peace Corps workers failing to fulfill their full commitment varied from eighteen percent in England to 100 percent for a hospital recruiting organization in the Middle East. The financial cost for these early returning people is considerable because the Peace Corps loses fifty to seventy-five percent of the $7000 it costs to recruit and train participants. Peace Corps volunteers face similar living conditions as missionaries serving overseas. However, Peace Corps volunteers are often younger and also usually commit to shorter periods of service, whereas missionaries often choose missions as their lifetime vocation. Storti gives further analysis concerning early returns from overseas assignments.

Storti found that the tragedy of those who fail and leave their overseas assignment is felt by the sending organization, by the people who return early, and by the people to whom they were sent. Storti says that the human cost for a missionary returning early is exacerbated by a sense of failure and loss of self-esteem. They have to undergo the stress of relocating again; their co-workers are left with bitterness, anger, a bunker mentality, and a reduction in their ability to show compassion. Storti identifies several reasons that new missionaries fail to survive their initial term of overseas service. They do not: (1) adjust to the initial move overseas; (2) adapt to the new culture in which they are suddenly immersed; (3) acclimate to a new climate with monsoons, floods, impassable roads, and mold growing on shoes, walls, and clothes; (4) get used to a life with poor communications and poor transportation; (5) learn to do without material

---

[1] Frank Allen, "Why Do They Leave? Reflections on Attrition," in *Evangelical Missions Quarterly* 22 no. 2 (April 1986): 118–121.
[2] Craig Storti, *The Art of Crossing Cultures* (Yarmouth, ME: Intercultural Press, 1990), xiv.

possessions; (6) cope with the fear of getting sick; and (7) learn to deal with loneliness, homesickness, and life without their traditional support group of friends and family.[3]

Storti suggests that missionaries fail because they do not adapt to stress. He makes seven suggestions about what can make missionary stress manageable.

1. Missionaries should be taught what to expect, because knowing what is coming helps diminish the impact these stresses have upon the individuals and their families.

2. Keep things in perspective by remembering the current stresses, such as sickness, are uncomfortable but not life-threatening.

3. Put things in perspective by remembering times while they were still in their home culture but were without family or friends, or when they moved or changed jobs.

4. Be positive in their attempts to establish themselves in the new country.

5. Exercise and get enough sleep.

6. Take the initiative to stay in contact with family and friends at home.

7. Seek out new friends in the new culture and cultivate those friendships.[4]

Storti's practical seven suggestions for stress management can be useful to missionaries on the field. These are areas that are often overlooked in the midst of stress. If followed, these suggestions help to avert early departures.

Another area of major stress is language acquisition and success in this area often affects longevity on the field. Language acquisition can be a stumbling block to a missionary's transition to life on the field. Storti says that learning the local language increases the foreign worker's effectiveness and speeds up cultural adjustment. Language acquisition develops: (1) a sense of well-being and security for the missionary; (2) a symbolic expression of affirming the national people's humanity and worth, helping to develop trust; and (3) the missionary's ability to engage local people and relax because he understands what is happening.[5]

Reasons for Missionary Longevity

Studies conducted on non-Assemblies of God missions sending agencies shed light on missionary attrition and longevity. This study will draw from some of the conclusions of these studies; however, my research is focused on Assemblies of God missionaries from the Asia Pacific region. Therefore, the Holy Spirit's role in the life of Pentecostal missionaries is added since these studies focus primarily on

---

[3] Craig Storti, *The Art Of Crossing Cultures*, (Yarmouth, Maine: Intercultural Press, Inc., 1990), 2–10.
[4] Ibid., 9–10.
[5] Ibid., 87–93.

material and psychological factors. Also, the study is limited to missionaries and cultural factors found within the Asia Pacific region.

A major study of missionary attrition is recorded in *Too Valuable to Lose,* edited by William D. Taylor. This study identifies problems experienced by sending agencies in older and newer sending countries for the years 1992 to 1994. Peter W. Brierley's chapter, "Missionary Attrition: The ReMAP Research Report" indicates that larger mission agencies have a higher rate of missionary retention. The overall results of the study reveal an average missionary loss of five point one percent per year. Attritional reasons identified in the study vary from the older to the newer agencies, making it difficult to formulate general reasons. However, the study did identify four unpreventable reasons for attrition: (1) retirement, (2) death of a spouse, (3) political crisis within the host country, or (4) marriage outside the mission. The study also identifies five personal and organizational elements of preventable missionary departure: (1) personal reasons, (2) marriage, (3) family, (4) societal, and (5) work related issues.[6] Brierley's five elements for preventable missionary departure are categories that are useful in this research, and his work is one of the sources I am using in my analysis.

Detlef Blöcher and Jonathan Lewis, in "Further Findings in the Research Data," reports that pre-field candidate screening and on-field training are effective ways to prepare missionaries. However, they did not identify retention methods because of the multiplicity of variables found while working cross-culturally.[7] They included helpful information for training missionaries.

William Taylor, in "Challenging the Missions Stakeholders: Conclusions and Implications; Further Research," offers foundational information on missionary training and its possible benefits. Taylor finds that missionary longevity is related to: (1) each missionary's individual spirituality; (2) relational skills that enable the missionary to avoid or mediate interpersonal conflicts; and (3) real ministry skills that are developed in a "pre-field" setting. Taylor also concludes that along with biblical, theological, and missiological training there should also be training on: (1) team relations, (2) significant involvement and interaction with supporting churches, (3) on-field care; (4) evaluation; and (5) closure.[8]

---

[6] Peter W. Brierley, "Missionary Attrition: The ReMAP Research Report," in *Too Valuable to Lose: Exploring the Causes and Cures of Missionary Attrition,* ed. William D. Taylor (Wheaton, IL: World Evangelical Fellowship Missions Commission, 1997), 86, 91.

[7] Detlef Blöcher and Jonathan Lewis, "Further Findings in the Research Data," in *Too Valuable to Lose: Exploring the Causes and Cures of Missionary Attrition,* ed. William D. Taylor (Wheaton, IL: World Evangelical Fellowship Missions Commission, 1997), 119.

[8] William D. Taylor, "Challenging the Missions Stakeholders: Conclusions and Implications; Further Research," in *Too Valuable to Lose: Exploring the Causes and Cures of Missionary Attrition,* ed. William D. Taylor (Wheaton, IL: World Evangelical Fellowship Missions Commission, 1997), 358.

Christopher H. Rosik and Jelena Pandzic, in *"Marital Satisfaction among Christian Missionaries: A Longitudinal Analysis from Candidacy to Second Furlough,"* did a study that followed twenty-eight missionaries from candidacy to the beginning of their second missionary term to see how their families were impacted during the first term of service. The missionaries were tested three times during this process with a Marital Satisfaction Inventory, which assessed ten dimensions of marital functioning. Repeated analysis showed that changes occur from candidacy to their first furlough. Both men and women were similar in their perceptions and marriage relationships changed in a negative manner towards their mate. The study revealed some unique stressors on missionary marriages:

1. Relocating to a new country stresses the whole family.
2. Culture shock affects women and men differently. Women's reaction can be seen in overeating, loss of sexual interest, crying, headaches, fatigue, and depression, while men, who are generally goal-oriented, find satisfaction in their work.
3. Financial concerns puts stress on a marriage.
4. Adolescent children in the home can also add to the stress felt in missionary marriages.

The results of their study revealed that member care should be a priority of missionary sending organizations, especially for first term missionaries who are entering parenthood or are raising young children.[9]

Several mission leaders detail reasons for missionary attrition that are beneficial to this project in the *Evangelical Missions Quarterly* (April 1986). However, none of the organizations listed are Pentecostal. Therefore, the pneumatological factor will not be included in their research, whereas this study will include aspects of being Pentecostal and the Spirit's influence upon missionary longevity. These leaders focused their research on the primary reasons missionaries left their work assignments and returned home.

First, Dave Camburn of the Conservative Baptist Foreign Mission Society, in "The Conservative Baptist Foreign Mission Society," says their research shows that the primary reason missionaries leave is the result of physical or emotional health problems. Other issues identified were family problems, conflicts on the field, poor administrative structures, personal unhappiness, doctrinal differences, or simply that they felt their work was completed.[10]

---

[9] Christopher H. Rosik and Jelena Pandzic, "Marital Satisfaction among Christian Missionaries: A Longitudinal Analysis from Candidacy to Second Furlough," in *Journal of Psychology and Christianity* 27, no. 1, (2008): 3–5.

[10] Dave Camburn, "The Conservative Baptist Foreign Mission Society," in Evangelical Missions Quarterly, 22, no. 2, (April 1986), 127–128.

Second, Burnis H. Bushong, a leader in the World Gospel Mission, says in his article titled, *"The World Gospel Mission,"* that their research identifies health concerns for family members as the primary reason for leaving. Other reasons were the desire to work with another mission or unsatisfactory educational opportunities for children on the field.[11]

Third, Michael Pocock, in *"The Evangelical Alliance Mission,"* collected what leaders of the Evangelical Alliance Mission sending organization claimed were reasons for missionary attrition. He lists health, marriage outside the mission, unilateral personal decisions, and dismissal.[12]

Fourth, Tim Ratzloff of the Christian and Missionary Alliance, reflected in *"The Christian and Missionary Alliance,"* that an evaluation of departures reflect that death, retirement, sickness, completion of their contract, transfers to North American ministry, personal and family problems, moral failure, and doctrinal deviations are reasons for early missionary departures.[13]

From these four sources there are similarities of reasons for attrition: personal reasons, marriage concerns, family issues involving stress in a new country and children's education, health, and work and finance issues.

Psychological Factors Involved in Missionary Longevity

Psychological factors impact the ability of missionaries to adjust successfully to a new cultural context, which affects their ability to successfully complete their first term of service. Understanding what these factors are and how they impact missionary longevity is important to the project.

Howard and William Hendricks, in *As Iron Sharpens Iron*, identify five motivational qualities in potential leaders that apply to missionaries. They show that people in missions often are: (1) goal-oriented, (2) initiators, (3) eager to learn, (4) willing to assume responsibility, and (5) willing to seek challenges and responsibility.[14] This information is applicable to this study as the motivations of candidate missionary's needs are assessed in pre-field training sessions.

Proper attitudes towards stress are important for missionary longevity. Marjory Foyle's *Honorably Wounded* contains a healthy approach to missionary attitudes as she focuses on the positive side of stress. She shows the difference between having

---

[11] Burnis H. Bushong, "The World Gospel Mission," in *Evangelical Missions Quarterly*, 22, no. 2, (April 1986), 129.

[12] Michael Pocock, "The Evangelical Alliance Mission," in *Evangelical Missions Quarterly* 22, no. 2, (April 1986), 122.

[13] Tim Ratzloff, "The Christian and Missionary Alliance," in *Evangelical Missions Quarterly* 22, no. 2, (April 1986), 125.

[14] Howard Hendricks and William Hendricks, *As Iron Sharpens Iron*, (Chicago, IL: Moody Press, 1995), 48–55.

some stress and feeling stressed all the time and indicates that stress can be a positive, motivating factor leading to action and success. Many missionaries at the end of successful missionary careers reflect that the stress points in their lives and ministries were key elements in their work success or attitude changes.[15] This information is important for the on-going training of both candidate and veteran missionaries as they encounter the stress of cross-cultural working, living, and family rearing.

Marge Jones and E. Grant Jones, in *Psychology of Missionary Adjustment*, identify variables that affect a missionary's ability to psychologically adapt to missionary life. They write that missionaries are often affected by decisions made beyond their control and with which they may not agree, so that their ability to maintain their self-confidence can be shaken. A fragile ego or rigid control mentality will hamper missionaries from being successful. Jones and Jones show that better adjusted missionaries are those who are more controlled, less moody, and more astute. Firstborn individuals, younger candidates, and those who score high on flexibility and perseverance are people who adjust better in cross-cultural settings. Their findings are important because, although God's call is important to the motivation and success of individuals, their future responses to stressful cross-cultural situations can be predicted by their behavioral history.

Their findings indicate that twenty to fifty percent of new missionaries do not return for a second term because in adjusting to a new cultural context, the missionary's achievement is affected by the stress of unrealistic expectations. There are five expectation pressures missionaries experience that may not align with reality: (1) self-expectations; (2) perceived national church expectations; (3) mission board expectations; (4) supporting church expectations; and (5) missionary colleagues' expectations.[16] The findings of Jones and Jones concerning unrealistic expectations is important in a missionary training program so that trainees can understand the importance of realistic expectations which will contribute to adjustment on the field.

Another issue identified by Jones and Jones relevant to this study is ethnocentrism, which is defined as an attitude of superiority that destroys personal relationships. They believe that cultural relativism is a healthier way of dealing with differences because it holds that all cultures are valid, but their validity may be experienced in different ways. Jones and Jones recommend developing an attitude of

---

[15] Marjory F. Foyle. *Honorably Wounded*. Sussex, England. (Evangelical Missionary Alliance, 1987), 14.

[16] Marge Jones and E. Grant Jones, *Psychology of Missionary Adjustment* (Springfield, MO: Logion Press, 1984), 20–22, 66.

mutual respect in order to combat ethnocentrism. This engenders attitudes in the missionary that are observable by members of the host country as the missionary becomes more acceptant and begins to seek the company of people from the indigenous culture.[17] Mutual accommodation can then be facilitated through training. This study will confront ethnocentrism by identifying social situations that may be difficult for new cross-cultural workers that can be addressed during pre-field and on-field training programs developed as a part of this project.

Jones and Jones include a description of a forty-hour training program developed by Assemblies of God missionary Ron Iwasko. After leaving the field, he served as personnel director for the Assemblies of God and was involved in the recruitment of new missionaries. The program was based upon eight important life questions.

1. How do I relate to the home office?
2. How can I manage daily living requirements?
3. How can I care for my family?
4. What ministry skills do I need?
5. How can I become effective in the new culture?
6. How should I relate to other missionaries?
7. How should I relate to the national church?
8. How should I react to non-Christian philosophies, practices, and forces?[18]

These questions are relevant to the training program developed to prepare men and women for missionary service before they go to the field and for on-going nurturing while they are working cross-culturally.

Culture Shock's Impact on Missionary Longevity

Another psychological difficulty confronting new missionaries addressed in this project is culture shock, which is an important factor in first term missionary attrition. Jones and Jones indicate that the level of culture shock is equal to the qualitative and quantitative differences between the value systems of their birth culture and the new culture where they are serving. They write that missionaries suffer from culture shock and stumble because they do not adjust to new life situations or become a part of the local culture. Their suggested remedy is for new missionaries to create an atmosphere in their home that is comfortable but does not become an American cocoon that isolates them from the local culture. Isolation

---

[17] Ibid., 54.
[18] Ibid., 24.

leads missionaries to become critical of the indigenous culture and hinders them from developing a sense of love for the local people. Culture shock hinders new missionaries from being willing to pay the price of adjustment, causing them to fail as missionaries, even though they may continue to stay on the field. This project will address the problem of culture shock in pre-field and on-field training.

Ted Ward, in *Living Overseas*, indicates that missionary life is an active and continuous process where people in cross-cultural ministry cope with new and different situations. Ward indicates that culture shock is a drawn-out process that is not the result of a specific event or a series of events, but it is the result of encountering new ways of doing things, perceiving realities, and understanding reality. He indicates that being without the cultural cues a person grew up with can be disconcerting. He suggests the missionary consciously try to develop an empathy with the culture where he is working and try to experience life from the point of view of others. Ward says this can help the missionary become shock resistant.[19]

A seminal work on culture and the church, which also deals with the difficulties of a person from one culture going to work in another, is *The Church and Cultures* by Louis J. Luzbetak. He writes that culture shock represents mental strain or physical exertion that can lead to missionary failure due to burnout, breakdown, exhaustion, collapse, or shock.[20] He identifies four stages of cultural adjustment that missionaries go through: (1) the tourist stage, (2) disenchantment, (3) resolution, and (4) adjustment. However, some modern missiologists do not accept all of these stages since some missionaries do not experience all of them because of the work they do. According to Luzbetak, all types of shock are similar and highlight the seriousness of culture shock by likening missionary culture shock to military battle fatigue. There are two terminal stages of culture shock as missionaries become apathetic to the culture or they have an atavistic response resulting in either going native or anti-native.[21]

Luzbetak identifies six symptoms that are indicators of culture shock: (1) increasing negativity on the part of the missionary and a suspicion of the people and their "ways"; (2) homesickness, loneliness, boredom, lethargy, and a tendency to withdraw; (3) rising stress along with a feeling of dissatisfaction, disgust, irritability,

---

[19] Ted Ward, *Living Overseas: A Book of Preparations* (Springfield, MO: Life Publishers International, 1984), 98–101.

[20] Louis J. Luzbetak, *The Church and Cultures: New Perspectives in Missiological Anthropology*, (Maryknoll, NY: Orbis Books, 1988), 203.

[21] Ibid., 217–20.

and depression; (4) physical sickness—headaches and hypertension; (5) excessive concern for one's health; and (6) alcoholic drinking or some other attempt to compensate for one's problems.

Of importance to the organizational aspects of dealing with people who develop culture shock are eight areas that require special sensitivity by mission leaders:

1. Physical adjustments to life in a new culture play a role in the overall adjustment of the missionary.
2. Interpersonal relationships can be painful as new missionaries attempt to find their way in relationships that are complicated by cultural roles and status.
3. Politeness and etiquette can be difficult for missionaries to learn as they struggle to understand what is proper and dignified in their new cultural context.
4. The use of space differs from culture to culture and the new missionary has to come to grips with the special understanding of distance between individuals and groups of people.
5. Cultures view the use of time differently.
6. Cultural incongruities or incompatibilities, such as how people dress (Luzbetak says this is like wearing tennis shoes with a tuxedo) or how people react to situations may confuse the missionary.
7. Verbal and non-verbal communication is one of the most serious aspects of a culture that produces culture shock.
8. Understanding the reasoning, reactions, and motivations of people in a different culture can create distress in new missionaries.

T. Wayne Dye's chapter, "Stress-Producing Factors in Cultural Adjustment," suggests six things to consider when helping new missionaries in the cultural adjustment stage:

1. Recognize the cultural stresses and do not deny them.
2. Escape through light reading, music, or some other hobby, and allow time for rest or recreation.
3. Decrease frustration by setting realistic goals.
4. Build acceptance through a study of culture in general and the new cultural context in particular.
5. Improve communication by studying the local verbal and nonverbal language.

6. Strengthen emotional security through your own self-acceptance.[22] This
    is of importance as the organization builds processes designed to help
    the leaders.

Craig Storti, in *The Art of Crossing Cultures*, describes the mechanism by which culture shock operates within the psyche of the new missionary. Culture shock begins with the missionary "pulling back" from the culture after an unpleasant encounter. Storti diagrams the process with three elements: (1) a cultural incident occurs; (2) causing a reaction—anger, fear, etc.; (3) which prompts a withdrawal.[23] To describe this process, Storti uses an example of a female expatriate worker in Tunisia who is intimidated by the aggressiveness of male customers at the post office. In isolation she might have dealt with this, but in the context of her continual experience with the crowds of pedestrians, streets choked with donkey carts and aggressive Tunisian taxi drivers, it caused her to pull back. Storti says that, "by withdrawing and isolating ourselves from the culture, we seriously undermine any possibility of meaningful adjustment."[24] Storti says as the withdrawal process accelerates the missionary ends up in "full flight" from the indigenous culture. The missionary either leaves or, if he is not willing to leave, he looks for alternative sources of social interaction by turning to the local expatriate subculture. These expatriate groups offer a sense of protection from the dominant indigenous culture as the missionary finds people with whom he finds much in common culturally. This leads the missionary into a mental state of a cultural malcontent.

Several authors contribute significantly to the understanding of what causes culture shock. Identifying these contributory components for the training processes developed in this research will help new missionaries survive their culture shock experience. Frances White, in *Some Reflections on the Separation Phenomenon Idiosyncratic to the Experience of Missionaries and Their* Children, identifies two types of separation that impact a missionary's culture shock:

1. Developmental, which is the natural progression from infancy to old age.
    This involves a departure from familiar sources of gratification as people
    engage in more age-appropriate methods of fulfillment and self-
    perception.

---

[22] T. Wayne Dye, "Stress-Producing Factors in Cultural Adjustment," in *Missiology*, vol. 2, no.1, (January 1974), 72–5.

[23] Storti, *The Art Of Crossing Cultures*, 29.

[24] Ibid., 28.

2.   Traumatic or unexpected separation involves geographic moves, illnesses, job changes, accidents, and disasters.[25]

G. Collins, in *You Can Profit from Stress*, identifies nine sources of stress encountered by missionaries during their first term of service in a new country: (1) loneliness; (2) pressure of adjusting to a foreign culture; (3) constant demands on one's time; (4) lack of adequate medical facilities; (5) overwhelming workload and difficult working conditions; (6) pressure to be a constant, positive witness to nationals; (7) confusion over their role within the local church; (8) frequent lack of privacy; and (9) inability to get away for recreation and vacation.[26]

Francis White's and Elaine Nesbit's article, *Separation: Balancing the Gains and Losses*, studies how missionaries cope with change and what effects it has on their ability to deal with culture shock. They identify four stages that affect how missionaries deal with change, separation, or loss:

1.   Denial. The new missionary minimizes the fact that she or he is in a new place for a term or a lifetime by writing home often and promising to return for important events. He or she thinks of the experience as if he/she were a tourist without the need to adapt to a new living environment.

2.   Anger. Anger manifests itself and is directed towards family or friends. It appears as impatience, gruffness, silence or criticism and can affect the missionary's adjustment.

3.   Sadness. This materializes as the missionary starts to realize the reality of his loss, which is caused by separation. This is called the "affective phase" that is typified by depression and despair.

4.   Resolution. As the missionary begins to accept his loss he begins to adjust to the new culture in a positive manner. He begins to live in the present and begins to integrate facets of his former life into his new context.[27]

Sherwood Lingenfelter's *Agents of Transformation: A Guide for Effective Cross-Cultural Ministry* identifies cultural bias as another contributing factor to culture shock. He says cultural bias will preclude the missionary from being successful in cross-cultural ministry. Lingenfelter uses Jesus as the ultimate model of adaptation to a new culture because the Incarnation allowed him to successfully deal with bias.

---

[25] Ibid.,31–32; Frances White, "Some Reflections on the Separation Phenomenon Idiosyncratic to the Experience of Missionaries and Their Children," in *Journal of Psychology and Theology* 11 (Fall 1983): 181–88.

[26] G. Collins, *You Can Profit from Stress*, (Wheaton, IL: Evangelical Missions Information Service, 1987).

[27] Francis White and Elaine Nesbit, "Separation: Balancing the Gains and Losses," in *Evangelical Missions Quarterly* 22 (October 1986): 392–98.

The ideal missionary mindset is one that strives for a "Pilgrim lifestyle" that disentangles itself from politico-economic social structures while staying morally and socially engaged.[28]

Everett M. Rogers' and Thomas M. Steinfatt's work, *Intercultural Communication*, provides further relevant information regarding bias. They describe bias as a form of "ethnocentrism," or a belief in the supremacy of one's own culture over another. They say that missionary success is hindered because of ethnocentrism. Rogers and Steinfatt recommend dealing with this in the training process by using experimental training within the new culture. This involves observing elements within a culture relativistically, with the entire culture in view. This will cause individual elements within a culture to make sense in light of their place within the greater culture. The purpose is to cause the cross-cultural worker to grow from an ethnocentric view of culture to an ethno-relativistic one. These secular suggestions do not lessen a missionary's call to transform the host culture into the image of Christ. Rogers and Steinfatt identify six steps in a process of ethno-relativism:

1. The missionary forms a parochial denial of cultural differences.
2. The missionary develops an evaluative defense against misunderstanding cultural differences as a threat to her own worldview.
3. The missionary begins to minimize cultural differences.
4. There is a gradual acceptance of cultural differences.
5. The missionary's thinking about cultural differences begins to change.
6. An integration of the differences occurs within the missionary's own worldview.[29]

This model mitigates the bias that can cause culture shock and impacts the missionary's long-term potential for success. In this book, I will target cultural awareness in pre-field and field-based training sessions as well as through the implementation of missionary mentors.

David Hesselgrave, in *Communicating Christ Cross-Culturally*, identifies cultural distance as a factor in missionary bias and ethnocentrism. He indicates this is also a causal factor in new missionaries encountering culture shock. Cultural distance, which is the gap between a missionary's culture and the host culture, affects how the

---

[28] Sherwood G. Lingenfelter, *Agents of Transformation: A Guide for Effective Cross-Cultural Ministry* (Grand Rapids, MI: Baker Books, 1996), 11–12, 231.

[29] Everett M. Rogers and Thomas M. Steinfatt, *Intercultural Communication*, (Long Grove, Illinois: Waveland Press, Inc., 1999), 221–27.

missionary filters information coming from his worldview, cognitive processes, linguistic forms, behavioral patterns, social structures, media influences, and motivational resources. Hesselgrave indicates that cultural distance leads to poorly trained missionaries who do not assimilate because they denigrate the host culture. This makes them susceptible to culture shock.[30]

Edward T. Hall's seminal work, *The Dance of Life: the Other Dimension of Time*, indicates that a missionary's perception of time plays a part in the understanding and acceptance of the local culture. Concepts of time are another contributing factor in missionary culture shock that is addressed by the project in pre-field training sessions. Hall indicates that the basic difference between the Western view of time and that of majority world people is how time is organized and used. Westerners usually are "monochromic," with a highly organized view of life who favor the goals of the organization. Monochromic time proponents tend to make a "fetish" out of time management. On the other hand, many majority world cultures are "polychromic," indicating a people-oriented mindset that has goals subordinated to the needs of people—not the organization. Polychromic cultures are usually autocratic and as functions increase, small bureaucracies proliferate. Missionaries have to recognize their monochromic predispositions and learn to accept the polychromic tendencies of majority world people who do not regard the clock on the same par as those from the highly organized West. Hall identifies differing categories of time that impact cultures differently.

1. Biological time is keyed to the ebb and flow of tides and seasonal rhythms.
2. Personal time is how people experience time in different contexts.
3. Physical time is based on the observation of the solstices and other physical phenomenon.
4. Metaphysical time is the paranormal view of time that looks into the future.
5. Micro time is a product of the primary level of culture.
6. Sync time describes people being "in sync" with the culture.
7. Sacred time, which American and European cultures have a hard time understanding, is a "mythic time" where past, present, and future coexist.
8. Profane time is rooted in the sacred time of the Middle East, which in turn grew out of physical time. Profane time marks minutes and hours, the days of the week, months of the year, years, decades, centuries—the entire explicit, taken-for-granted system that our civilization has elaborated.[31]

---

[30] David J. Hesselgrave, *Communicating Christ Cross-Culturally: An Introduction to Missionary* Communication, Second Edition (Grand Rapids, Michigan: Zondervan, 1991), 163–170.

[31] Edward T. Hall, *The Dance of Life: The Other Dimension of Time*, (New York: Anchor Books, 1980), 44–65.

The missionary's ability to adapt to different concepts of the passage of time and its relevance can play a crucial role in his adapting to the new culture. How to deal with this variable is included in the project.

Unrealistic Expectations and Missionary Longevity

Unrealistic expectations, as discussed earlier in the studies done by Jones and Jones, are a factor contributing to missionary attrition addressed in the project. An important work on this subject is Janice Dixon's Unrealistic *Expectations: The Downfall of Many Missionaries,* which says that one cause of missionary failure is naïve expectations of the work based upon a distorted self-image. A missionary believes he or she is God's answer to the problems of a particular field because the sending church thinks of the missionary as some type of super-person. Dixon says other difficulties that arise because of unrealistic expectations are:

- Frustration produced from faulty expectations developed before going to the new culture about their ability to adjust.
- Different living conditions than expected.
- Unexpected family problems.
- Misunderstanding their relationship with the national church.
- Disappointment with the spiritual level of national people because of their humanness, frailties, and weaknesses.
- Veteran missionaries who create stress because they are workaholics who demand the candidate learn everything quickly without help and guidance or times of spiritual refreshing together.[32]

Dixon believes missionaries should develop a "long-term view" of their position in God's mission and that it takes time to develop a fruitful ministry cross-culturally. Submission on the part of the missionary is essential to overcoming the false expectations of time.[33]

David Cummings, in *Programmed for Failure—Mission Candidates at Risk,* says that false expectations from being Americans can cause some missionaries to fail to adjust. He found that missionaries who do not overcome their American worldview will encounter trouble with their expectations about time their own independence causing them to not integrate into the broader missionary and national church

---

[32] Janice Dixon, "Unrealistic Expectations: The Downfall of Many Missionaries," in *Evangelical Missions Quarterly* 388–93, (no. 26, October 1990), 388–391.

[33] Ibid., 389.

community, and their expectation of institutional efficiency can cause problems. Another cause of missionary failure is the expectation of success found in new missionaries. They are from a culture where quick success based on formulaic approaches is lauded and failures are looked down upon. Cummings indicates that these false expectations lead to impatience, which ultimately produces discouragement and missionary failure.[34] Missionaries coming from non-Western cultures may not face exactly the same challenges, but they will have to deal with culture shock and dislocation.

Fred Renich, in *First Term Objectives*, deals with unrealistic expectations found in new missionaries. He lists six goals to which missionaries should aspire as they begin their career:

1.   Develop a good foundation in the language.
2.   Acclimate to the climate, customs, culture and people on their field.
3.   Acquire a thorough working knowledge of the mission.
4.   Learn the field, its problems, demands, and potential.
5.   Become self-aware of giftings and their place in the work.
6.   Seek a deepening confirmation of their call as a result of a sense of belonging and a consciousness of being useful.[35]

Renich contrasts these with four negative attitudes with which mission leaders will encounter in the new missionary recruits:

1.   New missionaries will experience a growing awareness of the shortcomings and weaknesses of their colleagues and mission leadership, which leads to distress.
2.   The destruction of new missionaries' idealistic view of the glamour of mission work will come to an end as they face the real work on the ground, which could lead to discouragement.
3.   The new missionaries' self-discovery may leave them aghast at what they find out about themselves, which could lead to failure.
4.   Mission leaders may find that the candidates they receive on the field will have weaknesses, making it necessary for mission leaders to continue learning about generational factors impacting the culturally bound recruits they receive.[36]

---

[34] David Cummings, "Programmed for Failure—Mission Candidates at Risk," in *Evangelical Missions Quarterly* 23, no.3, (July 1987): 240–46.

[35] Fred Renich, "First Term Objectives," in *Evangelical Missions Quarterly* 9, no. 3, (Summer 1967): 209–17.

[36] Renich, 209–17.

A helpful list for use in preparing new missionaries to survive their first term of service is found in Myron Loss' *Culture Shock: Dealing with Stress in Cross-Cultural Living*. Loss writes that to survive their first term of service, missionaries should: (1) set reasonable goals; (2) not take their job description too seriously; (3) be committed to joy; (4) maintain good emotional health; (5) remember they are human; (6) not be afraid of being a little bit eccentric; (7) be flexible; (8) not take themselves too seriously; (9) reduce their stress where possible; (10) make their cultural change gradual; (11) forgive themselves and others; (12) establish some close friendships with people from the host culture; (13) be thankful; (14) be encouragers; and (15) take courage because someone understands.[37]

Christopher H. Rosik's and Jelena Pandzic's study, *Marital Satisfaction among Christian Missionaries: A Longitudinal Analysis from Candidacy to Second Furlough*, identifies a variety of factors that cause personnel to leave the field. The most prevalent factors involved concerns for what occurs in families after relocating to a foreign culture. These include medical situations, children facing difficulties, or the needs of elderly parents. Their study followed twenty-eight missionaries from candidacy to the beginning of the second term to see how their families were impacted during their first term of service. The missionaries were tested three times during this process with the Marital Satisfaction Inventory developed by D. K. Snyder, and S. E. Costin, which assessed ten dimensions of marital functioning. Repeated use of the Analysis of Variance CANOVA analysis showed that changes occurred from candidacy to the first furlough. Both men and women were similar in their perceptions, and marriage relationships changed in a negative manner towards their mate.[38] This information is compared with the results of the project's study based on Asia Pacific first term missionaries.

The Call of God and Missionary Longevity

The lack of overall purpose is another factor that impacts missionary attrition. This is identified as a clear understanding of one's "call of God" for service in a cross-cultural ministry. The project will emphasize Jesus' words to the disciples, "You did not choose me, but I chose you and appointed you to go and bear fruit—fruit that will last" (John 15:16). This is foundational to the project's training of new missionaries

---

[37] Myron Loss, *Culture Shock: Dealing with Stress in Cross-Cultural Living*, (Winona Lake, IN: Light and Life Press, 1983), 85–101; Jones, Psychology of Missionary Adjustment, 71.

[38] Christopher H. Rosik and Jelena Pandzic, "Marital Satisfaction among Christian Missionaries: A longitudinal Analysis from Candidacy to Second Furlough," in *Journal of Psychology and Christianity*, Vol. 27, No. 1,(2008), 3–4.

because the Apostle Paul understood that he had been chosen to take the message of salvation to the Gentiles in other lands (Acts 22:21–22; Galatians 1:1–3; 2:6–7; 1 Corinthians 1:17; 9:16).

Os Guinness' *The Call: Finding and Fulfilling the Central Purpose of Your Life* is an important work that brings understanding of the dual sense of the call of God. The call to follow Christ is the primary and overarching call. But there is also another call to take the message of Christ to everyone, no matter where they may be found, that affects how we think, speak, live, and act. The secondary call is to various types of service, both secular and non-secular, for the glory of God. Guinness indicates that the missionary's challenge is to keep the right priority and order, because there is a danger of succumbing to the "Catholic distortion," which views vocational life as dualistic. This distortion places sacred or religious work in a primary position over those working in secular occupations, such as farmers or factory workers. Guinness says that all believers share the secondary calling and there is no distinction in service. He indicates there is a "Protestant distortion" as well that holds that only those in "full-time service" are called. In truth all are called to serve God "full-time" in whatever job or life's work they are engaged in. Guinness' concept that Christians are called to someone, not to some place, leads to a pious understanding of the missionary's identity and purpose through a relationship with God and not on a professional view of ministry or of culture.[39]

DeLonn Lynn Rance's *The Empowered Call: the Activity of the Holy Spirit in Salvadoran Assemblies of God Missionaries* sheds light on the call of Pentecostal missionaries. He says that vocation is an important aspect of the call of God for Pentecostals. God calls believers, according to Rance, to specific vocations for specific purposes. This vocational call motivates people for service and takes away lethargy. However, Rance indicates that not everyone is called to live cross-culturally in another country. The call is a work of the Holy Spirit, who does call some people to leave their home countries and take the gospel to another place. Rance believes this is essential for building the solid missionary foundation required for living long-term in a cross-cultural setting. The commitment to cross-cultural ministry is based upon a deep awareness of God's call and a desire to obey him in that call. It takes the motivation for obedience to a higher level than human determination and becomes a spiritual and an eternal calling from the heart of God to the heart of the person who recognizes he has been asked to do a specific work.[40]

[39] Os Guinness, *The Call: Finding and Fulfilling the Central Purpose of Your Life*, (Nashville, TN: Word Publishing, 1998), 31–43.

[40] DeLonn Lynn Rance, *The Empowered Call: The Activity of The Holy Spirit in Salvadoran Assemblies of God Missionaries*, (Pasadena, CA: Fuller Theological Seminary, 2004), 34–36.

Of special importance to the project is the understanding that the call of God is not derived from human strategies, but is a function of God's divine purpose. As such, the call of God is designed by God for his unique purposes. Rance points to the uniqueness of the call of God for a specific vocation as an important factor in missionary endurance. The sense of call draws a pious response to hardships in missionaries. The uniqueness is indicated because:

1. It is always God who calls.
2. God is holy and righteous, with a passion for social justice and fair dealing.
3. The tasks to which God calls people are endlessly varied and creative, and always unique and specific to the qualities and situation of the called person and to the circumstances of his time. Often it is a task that is for the freeing or liberating or empowering of others.
4. God selects people by his standards, which at first glance appears that he calls people who are unsuitable according to human standards.
5. There is always something unexpected about the call or how it is worked out because it draws on hidden facets found in the called person.
6. There is always a newness inaugurated by the fulfilling of the task, part of a journey to a new land.
7. The tasks are either beyond the capabilities of the called person or require special courage. They are things that are foolhardy to attempt in one's own strength, which requires the missionary's total dependence on God.
8. Usually the first reaction of the called person is a sense of inadequacy. If this feeling is not present to start with, it usually is later when the going gets rough. Sometimes the called person tries to evade the task.
9. The missionary task or assignment is not the missionary's personal possession in which he can take pride, but the converse—humility because it is God's work.[41]

David J. Hesselgrave's *Communicating Christ Cross-Culturally: An Introduction to Missionary Communication*, 2nd Edition focuses on missional communication, but Hesselgrave does indicate that the missionary's sense of calling is crucial to his long-term success and his commitment to learning the essentials necessary for cross-cultural communication. He connects the call of God for missionary service to the will of God. Hesselgrave shows that a commitment to missions involves obedience to the will of God. He shows how the apostles Peter and Paul persevered in their

---

[41] Rance, *The Empowered Call*, 34–35.

calling because they obeyed their Lord's will. This enabled them to keep their priorities straight and not be sidetracked by programs or instruments of missions. Their commitment to their call kept them focused on God's will and on people, which he indicates is what the church's mission is built upon and not programs, strategies, or methodologies. Hesselgrave says that it is the missionary's commitment to the person of Christ and the call of God that enables him to live a moral, ethical, and spiritual life that is the foundation of communicating Christ cross -culturally.[42]

Both Rance and Hesselgrave agree that a missionary's sense of calling and obedience to the will of God in fulfilling that call enables him to live a pure life and helps him face the hardships in missionary life. Rance points out that the uniqueness of the call of God for a special vocation is an important factor in missionary endurance. Hesselgrave stresses that a missionary's sense of calling is crucial to his long-term success and willingness to learn the essentials in cross-cultural communication.

Generational Factors and Missionary Longevity

This section will examine how generational factors impact missionary success. This is important because mission leadership is predominantly older and they find themselves engaging younger candidates who have a different worldview. The need to address generational issues is found in the statistics of the *Assemblies of God World Mission Annual Report of AGWM*, which reveal that the Assemblies of God U.S.A. has 2700 people working in over two hundred countries who are serving in two primary categories: (1) Career personnel who serve for three years or longer, with most in missions for a lifetime. (2) Missionary Associates who work cross-culturally for one or two-year assignments and are predominantly young. Additionally, more than 18,000 people went on short overseas trips of two to eight weeks in 2005, and they continue to provide a large resource group, some of whom will apply for associate and career ministry.[43] However, short-term mission experiences sometimes create unrealistic expectations that will need remediation if the person goes on to further, more permanent ministry in missions. Many of these short-term personnel are from the younger generation. These statistics reveal new missionary candidates, missionary associates, and short-term personnel bring generational issues that this project will address in the pre-field and on-field training sessions.

[42] David J. Hesselgrave, *Communicating Christ Cross-Culturally: An Introduction to Missionary Communication*, Second Edition (Grand Rapids, Michigan: Zondervan, 1991), 405.

[43] Assemblies of God World Missions. *Annual Report of AGWM*, (Springfield, MO: Gospel Publishing House, 2006), 2.

Paul McKaughan in *Missionary Attrition: Defining the Problem* provides pertinent information about why there is the need for missionary organizations to address generational issues. McKaughan indicates that there is a philosophical change occurring in the West that has impacted the younger generation's view of missions. He identifies some factors that cause this shift and are necessary for the project to include in the pre-field training process. McKaughan indicates that the world is smaller because of modern communication and travel, which decreases the distance between ministry in the home church and ministry abroad. Physical distance is no longer a deterrent, nor is it seen as a cause for missionary sacrifice.[44]

Second, openness and acceptance to cultures are essential. The younger generation has much greater openness and acceptance of other cultures. E-mail and the internet have given them greater knowledge and awareness of the world. Mass media has taught them to respect ethnicity, different cultural backgrounds, and religious beliefs. They are less likely to judge others just because they are different. Their own disillusionment with their world has created an openness to explore other world and cultural values. As a result, national patriotism and ethnocentrism are not big problems for them to overcome when crossing cultures.

Third, short-term missions are center stage in the mission's movement. Short-term missions is the choice of the new generation as they seek to experience other parts of the world. They have fewer funds but are willing to give financially and serve sacrificially when they believe in the mission. If they are committed to the vision they will find the time and funds to participate. This allows them to know the country better, meet the people, and become familiar with the mission which helps them know if they want to make a greater commitment.

Fourth, a friend approach to missions. Some in the younger generation recruit their friends to come with them into missions. They come in teams of four or more who go together for a single purpose. When they have a friend with them, or if someone is waiting for them on the field, they are more positive about going. This new generation is starting to impact missions with a fresh commitment and approach.[45]

---

[44] Paul McKaughan, "Missionary Attrition: Defining the Problem." in *Too Valuable to Lose: Exploring the Causes and Cures of Missionary Attrition*, ed. William David Taylor (Pasadena, California: William Carey Library, 1997), 15.

[45] Brian S. Burke, *How Gen X'ers are Changing the Face of Missions* [article on-line] (U.S.A.: The Network for Strategic Missions, 25 August 2000, accessed 3 July 2006); available from http://www.strategicnetwork.org/index. php? loc=kb&view =v&id=2776&fby=459&; Internet.

Factors Affecting Younger Applicants

This section will focus on student debt that often hinders young applicants from involvement in missions. Other factors are also included in this section such as moral/sexual failure, web-based pornography, conflict and lack of teamwork, lack of language learning and cultural adaptation which hinder them in successful mission work.

A generational reality for which the project must be prepared to engage is the debt the younger generation brings to their missionary careers. J. Wirt, S. Choy, P. Rooney, S. Provasnik, A. Sen, and R. Tobin, in *The Condition of Education 2004: Indicator 38: Debt Burden of College Graduates* show that the generation coming into the workforce from college in the year 2000 carried heavy debt. They show that nearly seventy percent of graduates with bachelor's degrees carried student debt into their early professional years, and according to the National Center for Education Statistics, this ratio is twenty-four percent higher than it was a decade earlier.[46]

Ben Sells, the former director of the International Centre for Excellence in Leadership at the Southern Baptist International Mission Board, defines the issue in *Student Debt: A Hurdle too high for "Impact" Missionaries*. He explains that student debt is an issue for people in public, private, and faith-based schools. The impact of debt on missions means that payments to maintain these debts become too large for missionary salaries.[47] While there is a growing desire among this younger generation to have a positive impact in missions as they recognize the world's needs, they are often relegated to the sidelines due to debt and cannot become impact missionaries.

Erich Bridges, in *Worldview: Debt: The Four-letter Word That Keeps Missionaries at Home*, deals with a number of issues that hinder the younger generations from being successful as missionaries. Occasionally, they leave the field because the Lord has directed them toward another ministry, and that is a positive reason. However, Bridges identifies eight impediments to missionary longevity that is of value in pre-field training sessions developed in this research.

First, the issue of debt for younger generation missionaries can be overwhelming. Bridges says that debt negatively affects the success of "impact"

---

[46] J. Wirt, S. Choy, P. Rooney, S. Provasnik, A. Sen, and R. Tobin, *The Condition of Education 2004(NCES 2004-077): Indicator 38: Debt Burden of College Graduates* [book on-line] (U.S. Department of Education, National Center for Education Statistics. Washington, DC: U.S. Government Printing Office, 2004, at <http://nces.ed.gov/programs/coe/2004/pdf/38_2004.pdf>, accessed 5 July 2006);

[47] Ben Sells, "Student Debt: A Hurdle too high for "Impact" Missionaries," *Missions Frontiers* (July-August 2004, (Pasadena, CA: Center for World Missions, 2004,), at <http://www.missionfrontiers.org/search.htm>, accessed 2 July 2007.

missionaries, which he defines as recent college graduates who make a significant contribution almost immediately. They are like "impact" athletes who become stars in their rookie season because even though they lack in maturity and experience, young workers more than make up for those in boldness, risk-taking, teachable attitude, and rapid language learning.

Second, unrealistic expectations can cause discouragement. Often new personnel have expectations of their own ministry that cannot be accomplished within the timeframe they have established. They may have expectations from others who have lived longer in the country or have served longer in a missions setting. Within most countries, the number of items that can be accomplished in a given time are far fewer than what was done before. Small irritations can grow in perspective until they have a major impact on the ability to function well in another culture.

Third, moral/sexual failings can destroy missionary lives, families, and careers. Web-based pornography heavily impacts the younger generation. Isolation can also open the door to wrong relationships. The onslaught of pornography has reached epic proportions, and anyone living on the mission field needs to have a variety of safeguards in place with clear accountability to fellow workers.

Fourth, personality and strategy conflicts can impact success. Recognizing there are various views by different age groups towards missions helps identify some causes of conflict. Various age groups have different backgrounds, priorities, world views, and degrees of patience. Some of those differences are generational and others are based on personality. Each must make an effort to understand the other's generational values. A lot of intergenerational communication is essential.

Fifth, failure in language learning and cultural adaptation can cause withdrawal from the people and mission failure. Humility, servanthood, and love can make up for many a shortfall in language study, Bridges stresses, but lack of commitment to effective, culturally sensitive communication sets mission work back in many ways. Unless a person is willing to immerse themselves into the culture, he or she will not understand many of the unseen but important values within the group of people where he or she is working. Cultural values are learned during language study and can be clarified if the missionary is observant to events and people he meets on a daily basis.

Sixth, lack of teamwork and pastoral care can lead to failure. Many mission agencies have addressed these critical flaws in recent years. The background and ministry experience of those applying for mission's appointment can reveal their readiness to become a part of a mission team. Short-term trips can help identify those individuals who understand and have developed their skills in group relationships.

Seventh, problems on the home front can distract from the work. One positive aspect of isolation on the mission field is distance from family conflicts, church splits and other problems back home. This is no longer true because missionaries are as close as the phone and the e-mail inbox, and can distract missionaries from the task at hand. Distance is no longer an issue when a family can vacation in the States for a reasonable cost. Too much communication with family and friends back home can distract the interests of personnel in their first term.

Eighth, Satan and his forces resist the work. Without overstating the devil's power, the reality that he resists missionary activity is known. This is why walking in the Spirit is crucial for younger missionaries adjusting to cross-cultural ministry. Paul's answer to the spiritual battle involved putting on the armor of God and being a person of prayer.[48]

The problem of student debt which relegates younger applicants to the sidelines is an important consideration and useful in my research analysis. Bridges' eight impediments to missionary longevity including moral/sexual failures, the problem of web-based pornography, conflict, lack of language learning and cultural adaptation and teamwork, too much contact with home front problems and spiritual warfare are all areas relevant for new applicants which must be addressed in pre-field training sessions. With these things in mind, we can now proceed to examining mission related organizational challenges.

---

[48] Erich Bridges, *Worldview: Debt: The Four-letter Word That Keeps Missionaries at Home*, (United States: SBC International Mission Board, Sep 07, 2004), available from <http://www.imb.org>, accessed 15 July 2007: 1–4.

3 CHALLENGES TO LONGEVITY

Organizational Factors Impacting Missionary Longevity

Although this study will concentrate on Assemblies of God missionaries, a look at other mission-sending agencies will provide a broader understanding of reasons for missionary attrition and longevity issues. A study by Eastern University's Douglas Trimble in Organizational Commitment, Job Satisfaction, and Turnover Intention of Missionaries evaluated job satisfaction and organizational commitment to longevity with retention among 468 missionaries and found that length of service related to job satisfaction was more important than generational factors in maintaining a committed missionary staff. Trimble concludes that missionaries are not blindly devoted to the organization but to their commitment to missions. The mission agency should have an organizational commitment to missionary job satisfaction and make intentional efforts to engender missionary job satisfaction.[1] Therefore, this section will examine some of the organizational factors that contribute to both longevity and attrition of missionaries. This is accomplished by looking at organizational principles that strengthen longevity in missions and missionary organizations.

Organizational Principles That Strengthen Longevity in Missions

In the book *Too Valuable to Lose*, principles that strengthen longevity in missions are highlighted in several chapters in an effort to minimize factors that cause attrition. One of the projects by William Taylor was called *Reduce Missionary Attrition Project* (REMAP). There were 110 participants from fourteen countries who met for the purpose of identifying factors that help missionaries not just survive but thrive within the culture where they were working.[2]

---

[1] Douglas Trimble, "Organizational Commitment, Job Satisfaction, and Turnover Intention of Missionaries," in *Journal of Psychology and Theology* 34 (Winter 2006), 349–60.
[2] William David Taylor, "Introduction: Examining the Iceberg Called Attrition," in *Too Valuable to Lose: Exploring the Causes and Cures of Missionary Attrition*, ed. William David Taylor. (Pasadena, CA: William Carey Library, 1997), 12.

William David Taylor, in Introduction: *Examining the Iceberg Called Attrition*, identifies factors that help keep personnel doing well in missions while living cross-culturally. Eight elements were identified that helped undergird effective longevity of service.

The first is spirituality. Total commitment to Jesus is critical to living in unfamiliar settings. Jesus said, "Follow me, and I will make you fishers of men" (Matt. 4:19, KJV). Following him comes before reaching others. Unless we have learned to follow him as faithful disciples, we cannot remain in difficult settings and retain effective ministry. There is an element of faith required at all times and in every situation. Faith is mentioned often in the Bible, and it must be combined with an attitude of submission to the Lord for effectiveness to occur. Jesus taught the disciples to "seek first his kingdom, and his righteousness."[3] I like the term "total abandonment." It speaks of not looking back but focusing on what he wants to do through our lives today and in the future. It says, "What I want comes secondary to what he wants and blends together with actively seeking to know what he wants to accomplish through us."[4]

Second is relational skills. This is another significant component that enables missionaries to stay in long-term mission work and be effective. Those who operate from a top-down perspective will have difficulty in other cultures. Interpersonal conflict has impacted many mission teams and caused some to leave. In addition to leadership skills, every person must also have follower skills.[5] Without an ability and commitment to encourage those around us, effectiveness in missions is limited. When we are concerned about the effectiveness of others, we often find they will in turn help us be more effective in our situation. The challenge of incorporating and blending together persons from different age groups who have varying backgrounds, values, and experience makes it even more critical to have good relational skills. The younger generations need to see exhibited among the older generations that teamwork and cooperation are still valued, and that example will help each succeeding generation more clearly see how God can work through the whole body.

The third element is ministry skills. Ministry skills are developed while on the job far more than while in an educational setting. During ministry a person can identify his greatest strengths and the areas with which he is most comfortable. As a missionary continues personal growth, he can see additional gifts emerge. Most

---

[3] Matthew 6:33.
[4] Taylor, "Introduction: Examining the Iceberg Called Attrition," 12.
[5] Ibid., 12.

people find it valuable to have some time of ministry in their own culture to better understand what the Lord is calling them to do.[6] National churches are maturing and continuing to develop their skills, and they need missionaries coming who have faced similar challenges and understand principles that help guide pastors and leaders in similar situations. To come alongside with encouragement and insights, missionary personnel need to understand many of the unique situations that can be faced in various ministry roles. This includes Bible School ministry, pastoral ministry, and the various leadership roles that need filling.

Fourth is training. The best attitude is one of a "life-long learner." There must be ongoing growth in various ways. This might include more formal educational training, short-term courses, and various practical programs.[7] As a mission organization, we encourage continued education and personal growth since they provide greater effectiveness long-term. This training can be in classroom settings, internet courses, or simple access to excellent books and magazines. Leadership development is a priority for effectiveness in every type of ministry, and the Asia Pacific regional leaders want our personnel to both enjoy learning and using the skills they learn to help develop others. Within Asia Pacific, national leaders put a high premium on higher education, and for missionaries to make a lasting contribution to these developing national churches, they must retain a student's heart.

Fifth is church involvement. The local church is foundational to spreading the gospel. We help plant local churches and strengthen leaders who will pastor those churches. The churches then have the biblical responsibility to send missionaries to other areas and support them with prayer, communication, and finances.[8] When there is good communication with the sending church and personnel living cross-culturally, there is greater commitment and longevity. Those who are approved for missions must have demonstrated an understanding of and commitment to the local church. After going to the field they must continue to strengthen and participate in church ministry, and in so doing they set an example to leaders and church attendees in every culture. One of the pillars of missions is the establishment and strengthening of local churches, and as church planting expands throughout the world, this will continue as a priority. It reminds us of Jesus' emphasis when he told the disciples he will build his Church and the gates of hell shall not prevail against it.[9]

---

[6] Ibid., 13.
[7] Taylor, "Introduction: Examining the Iceberg Called Attrition," 13.
[8] Ibid., 14.
[9] Matthew 16:18.

Sixth is on-field care. Field based member care is vital to long-term missions. If the personnel care is only from a distance there is a serious lack of close follow-up and adequate interaction. There is a need for accountability partners, field based personnel resources, and easy access to counseling and encouragement. Cross-cultural issues can create difficult situations that require immediate or ongoing assistance which can only be effective when help is nearby.[10] Proper member care includes mentoring of new personnel, good interaction by those living in one country, and occasional workshops that address relevant issues. The leadership of the Asia Pacific Region is fortunate to have a ministry called Missionary Renewal for Asia Pacific (MRAP) designed to assist in missionary care. One method used by MRAP is referred to as "transition and change" workshops. During these three-day workshops, personnel are able to address issues that impact them when change occurs. These changes can be transition to the States or back to the field, changes in ministry or family dynamics, children leaving for college, health issues, and numerous other change settings. These workshops are available several times each year both stateside and within an Asian setting.[11]

Seventh is evaluation. There is a need for regular self-assessment and leader-guided evaluation for missionary personnel. This can be a healthy way to grow and provide assessment. Evaluation makes a positive statement that leadership cares about the effectiveness and personal growth of each missionary. Evaluation can also provide the basis for identifying the need of ongoing training to address issues that hinder effectiveness. Younger generations today respond even more positively to evaluation than older generations. They recognize the need for ongoing assessment and work hard at improvement. Their desire for greater interaction provides an excellent platform to assist them in self-development and good assessment.

Eighth is closure. When closure does come it needs doing the right way with a healthy exit from missionary ministry. It can be retirement or transition to another type of ministry. Even when people leave missions for reasons other than retirement, it can be done in an effective and positive way that leaves good relationships for all who are involved.[12] Today's generation has a different perspective toward missions than past generations. Their commitments are more limited in time, and we see

---

[10] Taylor, "Introduction: Examining the Iceberg Called Attrition," 14.

[11] Missionary Renewal for Asia Pacific (MRAP) is based in Seattle, Washington and is led by Dr. Jack Rozell a missionary within the Asia Pacific Region. Dr. Rozell taught counseling at Northwest University prior to his appointment with AGWM. He along with his wife Adel previously pastored in Washington state.

[12] Taylor, "Introduction: Examining the Iceberg Called Attrition," 15.

greater attrition among younger generations during the first and second terms. Often these transitions back to the States are legitimate, and those involved agree that it can be best for the family and even the ministry. When that occurs, it is our desire to help them move forward into another effective area, and as we are able to assist, it usually helps them to continue making positive contributions in missions from new platforms of ministry.

Organizational Structures and Missionary Longevity

Taylor also addresses the cause and cure of missionary attrition. He calls attrition an "iceberg," meaning there is far more hidden below the surface than is easily seen from above. He sees backdrop areas that include pre-candidate components, training components, and field components.[13] This extensive work completed in 1997 continues to have valid information applicable for all mission organizations who desire to address issues of attrition and longevity. Philip Elkins and Jonathan Lewis, in *Attrition Tracking Guidelines for Mission Agencies*, provide a tracking guide for mission agencies that is a helpful tool for mission executives as they monitor field personnel and their ongoing wellbeing and effectiveness during each term. This will help during the development stage of this project as the ongoing development of missionaries is considered.[14]

Jim Van Meter, in *Five Strategic Suggestions for Increasing Retention*, makes suggestions to help a mission-sending organization increase its missionary retention. His examination of the issues is thorough and provides information that will relate directly to this project, especially in how mission executives engage missionaries and their involvement in the training process. Van Meter bases his suggestions on the best practices guidelines found in Conger, Alden, and Sullivan's Best Practices in Organization Development and Change. Van Meter suggests that the mission organization:

1. Determine what the retention rate is already in the organization.
2. Learn what the needs of the missionaries are.
3. Create a plan of action.
4. Train leaders and managers in member care.
5. Build in the process a system of accountability.

---

[13] Ibid., 5.

[14] Philip Elkins and Jonathan Lewis, "Attrition Tracking Guidelines for Mission Agencies," in *Too Valuable to Lose: Exploring the Causes and Cures of Missionary Attrition*, 371–376, ed. William David Taylor, (Pasadena, California: William Carey Library, 1997), 371–376.

Van Meter evaluated mission-sending organizations to determine what structures or operating principles contribute to longevity in missionary personnel. He concludes that sending agencies contribute to missionary longevity by identifying and addressing issues that lead to attrition. It is a conscious act on the part of the mission-sending organization to act as stewards and treat missionaries as valuable possessions in God's kingdom.[15] Van Meter says retention should be a priority for mission organizations because even agencies with good retention rates will lose about one percent of their personnel for preventable reasons. Preventable reasons are defined as people leaving for personal reasons, agency difficulties, work or team-related reasons, or dismissal. Unpreventable reasons occur because of retirement, death, illness, expulsion from the country, appointment to leadership positions, or visa problems.[16] Missionaries leaving average mission agencies have shown an increase in attrition over the past twenty years. From 1981 to 1985, one point sixty-nine percent of missionaries left for preventable reasons, while from 1996 to 2000, two point seventeen percent left. At the present attrition rate, an average agency will lose about forty-three percent of its personnel during a ten-year time span.

Van Meter found that denominational agencies had a higher retention rate (99 percent) than non-denominational organizations (96 percent). After analyzing all of the reasons why people left, it was determined that twenty percent left denominational agencies and sixty percent left non-denominational organizations for preventable reasons. Van Meter concludes that the closer the mission-sending organization is to the church, the greater the retention rate.[17] High retention rate agencies were evaluated and Van Meter identifies some areas where they differ from low retention rate sending organizations:

1. They emphasize the importance of pre-acceptance screening of applicants. All agencies screen applicants, but only the high retention agencies feel they are responsible to send only the ones who are "truly suitable."
2. They spend more time orienting the recruits to the organization. They spend at least six weeks in orientation versus three weeks for the low retention rate groups.

[15] Jim Van Meter, "Five Strategic Suggestions for Increasing Retention," in *WEA Resources*, at <http://www.wearesources.org/PublicationDetail.aspx?PublicationGUID=51ca8c38-d984-4d34-a0d6-a0acf5920518>. Accessed June 22, 2008.

[16] Ibid., 29.

[17] Jim Van Meter, "Distinctive Practices in High Retention USA Agencies," in Connections: *The Journal of the WEA Missions Commission*, (June–September 2004), 26.

3. They emphasize clear communication of plans and job descriptions. There is a communication from the leaders, between the churches and the field, and missionaries are included in major field decisions.
4. They actively promote a culture of prayer. All agencies mention prayer, but high retention agencies are more active in communicating and carrying through.
5. They provide on-field and on-going training for missionaries on the field. They do this in the area of language training and the development of ministry gifts and skills.
6. They place more emphasis on reaching the unreached (less than one percent are Christians). This is determined by the percentage of personnel who are working with the unreached. High retention rate agencies allocate thirty-one percent to these people, while low retention rate groups allocate twenty percent.
7. They give a greater percentage of missionary support to retirement. Nine percent for high retention and six percent for low retention agencies.[18]
8. Van Meter found that large sending organizations did the following things well. They provided: (a) provisions for handling complaints; (b) annual performance reviews; (c) satisfactory schooling for missionary's kids; (d) healthcare; (e) risk assessment with contingency plans; and (f) formal debriefings during furloughs.[19]

Van Meter makes the following suggestions for mission agencies that are pertinent to the project that focuses on developing missionary longevity in the Asia Pacific region: (1) Develop closer relationships with local churches; (2) improve the screening process; (3) develop good communication practices; (4) develop a good orientation process; (5) learn the needs of missionary personnel; and (6) understand the reasons why missionaries leave.[20]

Kelly O'Donnell writes about the importance of healthy missions in *Missionary Care, Counting the Cost for World Evangelization*. One chapter titled "The Dynamics of Healthy Missions" addresses criteria that are essential for missions to remain strong and balanced in the midst of change. For missions to remain strong there must be an emphasis on the whole and not just the individual situation. A holistic approach provides a better way to see how the individual parts are integrated

---

[18] Ibid., 27–8.
[19] Van Meter, "Distinctive Practices in High Retention USA Agencies," 28.
[20] Ibid., 28–9.

together. All mission organizations have several components which include the field-based personnel, leadership structure both on the field and home base, the overall mission organization, as well as the sending body and national church where they are sent. O'Donnell lists five areas that organizations can assess themselves as they evaluate the health of their program. These questions are of benefit as this project is developed: (1) Are there cohesive networks that allow individual uniqueness while providing a sense of unity within the whole? (2) Do patterns and boundaries provide clear structured flexibility without rigidity? (3) Does the organization provide stability during transition because of its adaptability? (4) Do the mission regulations give enough flexibility to allow easy monitoring and the ability to organize smoothly as it fulfills its objectives? (5) Does the organization communicate clearly and openly, and is it responsive and interactive?[21]

O'Donnell also deals with member care in *Going Global: A Member Care Model for Best Practice*. He discusses the ethical aspects of a mission sending organization's responsibility for taking care of its members. He says that this task is a challenge because of the resources that are required.[22] Raising awareness of the need for member care among certain sending churches and agencies that overlook or misunderstand its value is another challenge. Some smaller organizations may find it onerous but the sharing of resources between agencies can help. O'Donnell suggests periodic reviews by sending groups of their member care to evaluate the following issues:

1. Is there accessibility of care to the members and does it meet the needs of the people?
2. Does the organization build member care functions that enable people to feel supported and enriched spiritually? Are these care systems sustainable and do they provide comprehensive resources?
3. How does the organization network with others?
4. Has the organization identified its guiding principles and priorities?[23]

O'Donnell approaches member care through a model that contains five spheres and five best practices. This model is relevant to this research as part of the focus that will analyze Asia Pacific's organizational structures in training and missionary nurturing processes. From this analysis we will develop some best practices for use in

---

[21] O'Donnell, Kelly, *Missionary Care: Counting the Cost for World Evangelization*, Pasadena, CA: William Carey Library, 1992, 235–244.

[22] Kelly O'Donnell, "Going Global: A Member Care Model for Best Practice," in Doing Member Care Well: Perspectives and Practices From Around the World, 13–22. ed. Kelly O'Donnell, (Pasadena, CA: William Carey Library, 2002),.

[23] Ibid., 20–21.

the region's training endeavors. O'Donnell's five spheres contain a "best practice" principle that relates to the "flow of care" that is required for longevity.

1. The flow of Christ. This is where the member receives care from Christ and in return expresses care for the Master.[24]

2. The flow of community. This occurs as the members take care of themselves and receive care from the expatriate communities, which O'Donnell calls the "backbone of member care."[25] He indicates that social support is a critical key to missionary adjustment.

3. Sender care—the flow of commitment. This involves the sending organization's commitment to care for its members through every stage of the process, from the missionary's candidacy to retirement.

4. Specialist care—the flow of caregivers. This is care by specialists who are "professional, personal, and practical."

5. Network care—the flow of connections. Care and resources for the members are delivered through networks that facilitate member care.[26]

The summer 2008 *Enrichment Journal* is devoted to the growth of the Assemblies of God World Missions and the growing number of mission personnel, candidates applying for appointment, and worldwide constituency. Two articles in particular are of importance to the project. First, Russ Turney, Richard Nicholson, Mike McClaflin, and Ron Maddux, in *The Four Pillars of Missions Strategy: Reaching, Planting, Training, Touching*, articulate the priorities of the Assemblies of God. They describe the missional purposes of reaching the lost, planting the church, training leaders, and responding to the hurting with ministries of compassion. Each pillar is connected to the others, and this provides great variety of holistic ministry opportunities. Understanding this is crucial to developing a training regimen for missionaries in this project.[27]

Second, George O. Wood, in *My Five Core Values*, explains the core values that he operates under as General Superintendent of the Assemblies of God. It is important to have these clearly articulated because they have become the core values that drive the U.S. Assemblies of God in this current era. This project will assimilate these values and communicate them to the missionary body through its training and missionary renewal sessions as developed in the project.[28]

---

[24] O'Donnell, "Going Global," 17.

[25] Ibid., 17.

[26] Ibid., 16–19.

[27] Russ Turney, Richard Nicholson, Mike McClaflin, and Ron Maddux, "The Four Pillars of Missions Strategy: Reaching, Planting, Training, Touching," in *Enrichment Journal*, vol. 13, no. 3, summer 2008, 55–64.

[28] George O. Wood, "My Five Core Values," in *Enrichment Journal*, vol. 13, no. 4, Winter 2008, 16.

The AGWM has eight core values that can give missionaries a sense of purpose, which can be especially helpful in times when they question their reason for being on the field and are tempted to leave:

1. A biblical understanding of the mission of the church.
2. The principles of the indigenous church and partnership.
3. Knowing the culture, language and world view of those people with whom we work.
4. Practicing spiritual disciplines for personal spiritual formation.
5. The team concept of working together as missionaries.
6. Proclaiming the gospel to unreached people.
7. Holistic missions in word, deed and spirit.
8. Fulfilling our mission in the power of the Holy Spirit in word and deed.

These values taught to new missionaries and reinforced in veterans, will eventually become part of the missionary's personal value system. As they struggle with the pressures of cross-cultural missionary work, these values give them a foundation upon which the pressures are addressed.

M. Elizabeth Lewis Hall, Keith J. Edwards, and Todd W. Hall, in *The Role of Spiritual and Psychological Development in the Cross-Cultural Adjustment of Missionaries,* describe a study of 181 missionaries from forty-six countries to determine the relationship between spiritual development and both psychological development and cross-cultural adjustment. This study is of value to the project because a part of the on-going training in the annual missionary renewal sessions will focus on psychological health as well as cross-cultural adjustment. The hypothesis of the authors is that spiritual development was associated with psychological development and socio-cultural cross-cultural adjustment. They believe that spiritual development contributes to the adjustment of missionaries beyond what normally is credited to just psychological adjustment. Their basis for understanding spiritual development in the individual was to assess the degree that a missionary's relationship with God reflected their ability to have an emotional connection with him in times of trouble and stress. They used the Spiritual Assessment Inventory (SAI; Hall & Edwards, 1996), which is designed for clinical and research use. It included 54 questions where the missionary rated his relational patterns with, and spiritual awareness of, God. It utilized a five-point Likert scale that ranged from "not true at all" to "very true."

Hall, Edwards, and Hall concluded that spiritual development is related to psychological development. The study's implications for mission-sending organizations are that missionary spiritual development leads to adjustment on the field, which contributes to longevity of service. The results indicate that sending organizations should provide pastoral and psychological support for missionaries during candidate screening and throughout their careers. This will improve missionary adjustment and longevity. The findings also indicate that care should be taken during the candidate screening process to identify people with psychological needs because people who do not have adequate psychological resources are at risk of not being able to adjust adequately. People with an ambivalent relationship with God will experience difficulty in dealing with hard times. Their conclusion was that early identification of psychological or spiritual relationship needs might lead to early efforts to help and prevent suffering and missionary attrition.[30]

Dave Broucek, one of the presenters at the 2004 National Missionary Trainer's Forum, presented a paper about best practices and missionary training titled, *Best Practice Standards for Missionary Training*. He said that missionary training should form some best practices standards in missionary training as formal schools do for training regular students. He proposed that missionary sending organizations should also be missionary training and equipping organizations. In order for the organization to adequately train missionaries to cope in their new environments, the organization needs a "voluntary, ongoing, noncompetitive process of self-assessment, benchmarking, continuous improvement, and external evaluation that leads to outstanding performance."[31] He lays out steps the organization can take to ensure it adheres to the best practices that he takes from the Malcolm Baldrige National Quality Program, created by the U.S. Congress as a voluntary program to develop organizational excellence. The steps are:

1. Self-assessment. The first step is writing an Organizational Profile, which is a snapshot of the mission-sending organization that describes the organization's operations and challenges. This can be a growth experience in itself. "Self-assessment can provide an impetus for learning, a stimulus for growth, and a trigger for action."

---

[30] M. Elizabeth Lewis Hall, Keith J. Edwards, and Todd W. Hall, "The Role of Spiritual and Psychological Development in the Cross-Cultural Adjustment of Missionaries," in Mental Health, Religion & Culture April 2006; 9(2), 193–208.

[31] Dave Broucek, "Best Practice Standards for Missionary Training," in "Toward Best Practices in Missionary Training," in *Next Step: The North American Partnership in Mission Training*, 75–88, May 2004, at <http://passionexchange.wordpress.com/missions-resources/>, accessed April 4, 2010, 75, 83.

2. Benchmarks of excellence. The Baldwin process asks eighty-five questions in seven categories, which become the criteria for excellence in the organization.

3. Continuous improvement. The process occurs again over time to see how the organization is improving in the areas in which it wishes to excel.

4. External evaluation. The Baldwin process uses an external panel to assess the organization's improvement.[32]

Broucek adds two elements to the Baldwin process in order to align it with mission organizations. He says their assessment model should be voluntary in nature because mission-sending bodies have enough stress and do not need new bureaucracy. They should also be non-competitive. Whereas the Baldrige process is competitive in nature, the church is better served by operating in cooperation with other mission organizations for the advancement of God's kingdom.[33]

Geoff Tunnicliffe, in *Code of Best Practice in Member Care*, examines the Evangelical Fellowship of Canada's written code of best practices for their member care used to prepare their missionaries to adapt to life abroad. The code is based on their core values that include commitments to: (1) dependence on God for wisdom, power, and love in all aspects of member care; (2) the total well-being of cross-cultural workers; (3) helping them minister effectively, while recognizing the possible hazards, stresses, and sacrifice inherent in cross-cultural life and ministry; (4) the biblical ideal of the Body of Christ working together, through the church, mission organizations, and other partnerships; (5) the appropriate utilization of all available resources; (6) encouraging organizations to practice care of their members with consistency, excellence, and high standards of ethical, spiritual, and moral responsibility.[34]

Their code of best practices is developed in six categories:

1. Four principles of organizational policy and practice. (a) Member care policies are for all members. (b) Members participate in the development of the policies. (c) Agreed-upon personal and organizational beliefs and conduct are essential to effective care. (d) The organization is committed to developing member care that enhances kingdom ministry.

2. Seven principles of selection, training, and career care. (a) Candidate selection that is thorough and fair and also considers the roles of men and

---

[32] Ibid.

[33] Ibid.,84–86.

[34] Geoff Tunnicliffe, *Code of Best Practice in Member Care*, (Surrey, BC: Evangelical Fellowship of Canada, 2001), 1.

women. (b) Assignments are based upon expertise, giftedness, developmental stage, strengths and limitations as much as possible. (c) Providing appropriate training and professional support. (d) Realistic work expectations. (e) Personal renewal. (f) Endurance strategies are articulated and provided. (g) Care for the missionary beyond their field ministry to include furlough, re-entry, re-deployment (if it occurs) and retirement.

3. Two principles of community life. (a) A commitment to the idea that healthy Christian communities contribute to personal growth and ministry effectiveness. (b) Member care is personal, mutual, and organizational.

4. Two principles of family and missionary children care. (a) Missionary effectiveness is related to the holistic care of the family. (2) The sending church is a part of the process of care for missionary children.[35]

5. Missionaries should have personal relationships with churches. The local sending church should be a part of the missionaries' "continuum of care."

6. Crisis and contingency care. Procedures should be in place to help missionaries in a variety of contingencies. This includes crisis situations, dealing with moral failure, and discipline. There should be a disciplinary process defined as well as a process of restoration.[36]

C. David Harley, in *Preparing to Serve: Training for Cross-Cultural Mission*, stresses a holistic approach to missionary training that seeks to prepare candidates emotionally, mentally, spiritually, and practically so that they might be successful in adapting and working in a new culture. To do this he prioritizes the training components. In his research he analyzed six Two-Thirds World missionary training programs to determine the prioritized list.

1. Spiritual development. Four of the centers responded that this was a high priority, but they all said that they struggled to find an appropriate way to do this. They found that offering a course on spiritual warfare helped students come to grips with spiritual matters, especially when it was accompanied with some type of mentoring.

2. Character development or learning to live as Christians with others in community. "Missionaries must not only preach about the love of God;

---

[35] Tunnicliffe, *Code of Best Practice in Member Care*, 3.
[36] Ibid., 2–7.

they must demonstrate the love of God in their lives. They must not just talk about Jesus; they must reflect His character. Missionary candidates need to appreciate that people are attracted to Christ more by the lives of Christians than by their words."

3. Practical development and developing a personal perspective on mission. This is done through various practical courses that include dealing with culture, ministry strategy, and leadership.

4. Ministry skill development and learning how to evangelize cross-culturally.

5. Developing ministry effectiveness in both single and married missionaries by addressing issues unique to both in cross-cultural settings. This also involves teaching on cultural issues and also interacting through discussions on topics that may create cultural stress and lead to a failure to assimilate. These topics can include being single and pressures that may arise and also stresses that may occur in marriages and the challenge of raising "third-culture" children.[37]

R. P. Meyers and J. P. Tett, in *Job Satisfaction, Organizational Commitment, Turnover Intention, and Turnover: Path Analysis Based on Meta-analytic Findings*, recognize a correlation to longevity of service to job satisfaction as well as commitment to the organization. Linking ministry needs with a missionary's gifting and interest is important for ongoing satisfaction.[38]

Jim Van Meter, in *Ideas for Increasing Missionary Retention within Your Organization*, compiled information from a 2004 conference in Richmond, Virginia, where 180 attendees from fifty mission-sending agencies addressed two questions about "Strategies for Retention." The first question was, "What are some of the key things that need to happen to increase the likelihood of our missionaries staying longer with their agency?"[39] Ten groups discussed this and were asked to list the top five areas of concern. The summarized results show that the attendees were concerned with:

1. Ongoing spiritual formation and development with an emphasis on the missionary's identification being "in Christ" rather than in the culture and an understanding of a biblically-based call.

---

[37] C. David Harley, *Preparing to Serve: Training for Cross-Cultural Mission*, (Pasadena, CA: William Carey Library, 1995), 79–91.

[38] R. P. Tett, and J. P. Meyer, "Job Satisfaction, Organizational Commitment, Turnover Intention, and Turnover: Path Analysis Based on Meta-analytic Findings," in *Personnel Psychology*, 46, (260), 1993.

[39] Jim Van Meter, "Ideas for Increasing Missionary Retention Within Your Organization," in *World Evangelical Alliance* Web site, available from http://www.wearesources.org/ Publication Detail. aspx?PublicationGUID=51ca8c38-d984-4d34-a0d6-a0acf5920518, accessed June 22, 2008

2. Ongoing training and development through continuing education that is holistic and includes team dynamics, interpersonal skills, and conflict resolution.
3. Entry orientation that includes language and culture skills, mentoring, addresses clear expectations, and couples effective pre-field orientation with training.
4. Member care that is proactive and includes preventative care, family issues (kids in college and becoming grandparents), and pastoral care through the life-cycles of missionaries.
5. Personnel and human resource decisions that place people in positions that align with their ministry gifts and skills, screens appropriately, and relays realistic information so new missionaries arrive with realistic expectations.
6. Leadership and management practices that develop leadership skills in missionaries, help them understand the concept of servant leadership, nurture two-way communication, allow for missionary creativity, offer an accurate job description, and accountability that minimizes mission politics and favoritism.[40]
7. Resilient missionaries are needed who see themselves as productive and effective.
8. The missionary should have a relationship with the sending churches so they are accountable.
9. A culture within the organization is crucial where personal empowerment and development is encouraged, where the core values of the organization are communicated, prayer is deemed important, and the organization has a servant attitude.[41]

The conference then addressed the question, "What are some of the hurdles we will need to overcome as Human Resource people, in order to take the actions we have just discussed?"[42]

1. Resources were seen as essential and should consider the cost, time, and personal limitations of the missionary body.
2. The organization should make retention a priority.
3. Be considerate of missionary "mid-career" life transitions.

---

[40] Van Meter, "Ideas for Increasing Missionary Retention Within Your Organization," 1–2.
[41] Ibid., 2.
[42] Ibid., 2.

4. Work to overcome "spiritual blockage" and encourage people in matters of spiritual formation.
5. Communicate to the missionary body any changes occurring and make sure there is "buy in" by field leadership.
6. Leadership vision about member care must be communicated to those on the field.
7. There must be an organizational culture that emphasizes the team and not just the task, being flexible and open minded about trying new things, and willing to deal with hard issues, including gender roles.[43]

According to the Assemblies of God World Missions' report that covered the years 2001 to 2005, within the U.S.A. more candidates are applying each year for a career in missions than in the history of this fellowship. The average number of approved candidates exceeded 120 per year during that five year period. This is also true for the associate category and short-term teams as each grows annually.[44]

From the data provided by the above sources on organizational contributions to longevity, the areas of spirituality, relational skills, ministry skills, training which includes leadership development, church involvement both at home and abroad, field member care and evaluation were some of the areas in which the sending organization can help to ensure longevity. Van Meter suggested determining the retention rate of the mission organization, assessing missionary needs and developing an action plan that included training and accountability. Broucek outlined a plan including self-assessment of the organization as well as external evaluations, finding the organization's benchmarks of excellence and determining to have continuous improvement. Several authors stressed that mission organizations must make retention a priority and develop an organizational culture that emphasizes the team.

Mentoring and Its Contribution to Longevity

An important factor in new missionary longevity is mentoring. An important book in this field is Bobb Biehl's *Mentoring: Confidence in Finding a Mentor and Becoming One*, which stresses the difference a mentor can make in the life of those are mentored. Biehl explains that mentoring and discipleship are associated, but differ slightly in focus with the necessity for developing leaders being crucial in the mentoring process. Biehl indicates that in the mentoring process the person who is

[43] Van Meter, "Ideas for Increasing Missionary Retention Within Your Organization," 3–4.
[44] Assemblies of God World Missions. *Annual Report of AGWM*, (Springfield, MO: Gospel Publishing House, 2006), 2.

mentored is taught to make decisions about what to do in a situation, why certain courses of action are important, and how to use available resources.[45]

Mentoring is not a modern missional construct developed from organizational sciences. It was practiced by Jesus, as revealed in the gospels. Jesus is shown as a successful mentor by Paul Stanley and J. Robert Clinton in *Connecting: The Mentoring Relationships You Need to Succeed in Life*. They evaluate mentors according to the criterion of discipler, teacher, spiritual guide, coach, counselor, sponsor, contemporary model, and historical model. Stanley and Clinton say that (1) Jesus was a discipler because he taught those who listened how to live disciplined lives. (2) He was a teacher (Matt. 10:24; 17–23, 26–42) as demonstrated by his parables and he constantly revealed the meaning of the Old Testament in relation to himself and God's purposes for creation. (3) He was a coach as he instructed and then sent his followers into ministry. (4) He was a spiritual guide, which was revealed by how he demanded maturity and accountability. (5) He sponsored his followers in the Kingdom of God, which allowed them to experience the glorious Pentecostal experience of the upper room. (6) He was a counselor through his dealings with them in relation to God's kingdom.[46]

David Stoddard, in *The Heart of Mentoring*, addresses the mentoring relationship and lists ten principles of effective mentoring. He says that effective mentors understand that living is about giving; they see mentoring as a process that requires perseverance; they open their world to their mentoring partners; they help mentoring partners align passion and work; they are comforters who share the load; they help turn personal values into practice; they model character; they affirm the value of spirituality; they understand that mentoring that leads to reproduction creates a legacy of good leadership; and they are committed to action. He describes mentoring as a long-haul process that requires perseverance but enables people to determine their priorities, clarify their passion, and address their pain. Mentoring focuses on changing people on the inside and involves the spiritual side of a person.[47]

J. Robert Clinton and Richard W. Clinton, in *The Mentor Handbook: Detailed Guidelines and Helps for Christian Mentors and Mentorees*, discuss mentoring models that involve active mentoring, occasional mentoring, and passive mentoring. Active

---

[45]Bobb Biehl, *Mentoring: Confidence in Finding a Mentor and Becoming One*, (Nashville, Tennessee: Broadman and Holman Publishers, 1996), 122, 145.

[46]Paul D. Stanley and I. Robert Clinton, *Connecting: The Mentoring Relationships You Need to Succeed in Life*, (Colorado Springs, CO.: NavPress, 1992), 42–43.

[47]David Stoddard, *The Heart of Mentoring*, (Colorado Springs, Colorado: NavPress Publishing Group, October 2003), 11–12, 211.

mentoring is the more focused and intentional of these models, and it requires the greatest amount of commitment and time. Each of these models includes five underlying factors that determine the effectiveness of the process. These factors include a respect for the mentor that is earned by his or her effective life, relationships that develop into a two-way bond of trust, responsiveness by both parties to the mentoring process, accountability that keeps the process on track, and empowerment.[48]

Laura Raab and J. Robert Clinton, in *Barnabas, Encouraging Exhorter: A Study in Mentoring*, promote Barnabas as an ideal example for mentoring because he mentored Paul and Mark. Both men had a greater impact upon the world than Barnabas, with Paul founding many churches and Mark authoring part of the New Testament. Barnabas' positive influence helped guide them into greater ministries.[49]

Steffen and Douglas, in *Encountering Missionary Life and Work: Preparing for Intercultural Ministry*, recognize the importance of having competent coaching for culture and language acquisition. They see the value in both effectiveness and enjoyment, especially when a native speaker who knows the culture provides extended time for mentoring and coaching.[50]

The Asia Pacific Region has encouraged a mentoring relationship between new personnel and selected veterans who have demonstrated a positive outlook and have worked well with fellow missionaries and national leaders. In countries where there are multiple workers, capable veterans are assigned to meet periodically with new personnel to address pertinent topics like cultural adjustment, culture shock, relationships with mission team members and the national church, communicating with supporters and the national office, and various other subjects as the need arises. In some cases, one of those subjects is conflict management, which is the subject of the next chapter.

---

[48] J. Robert Clinton and Richard W. Clinton, The *Mentor Handbook: Detailed Guidelines and Helps for Christian Mentors and Mentorees*, (Altadena, California: Barnabas Publishers, 1991), 2–14.

[49] Bobby Clinton and Laura Raab, *Barnabas, Encouraging Exhorter: A Study In Mentoring*, (Altadena, California: Barnabas Publishers, 1997).

[50] Tom Steffen and Lois McKinney Douglas, *Encountering Missionary Life and Work: Preparing for Intercultural Ministry*, (Grand Rapids, Michigan: Baker Academic, 2008), 139.

4 INTERPERSONAL CONFLICT AND SPIRITUAL FACTORS THAT IMPACT MISSIONARY LONGEVITY

A major component of the training processes is conflict management between missionaries, cross-culturally between the missionary and the national church, and being a peacemaker within the national church.

Hugh Halverstadt's *Managing Church Conflict* is an excellent manual for managing conflict in the church that is applicable to the missional context and for training new and veteran missionaries. Aspects of it are applicable to this project that will include conflict management in the training program. Halverstadt states that conflicts are the result of power struggles over differences—differing information, beliefs, interests, desires, values, or abilities to secure needed resources. He approaches conflict resolution from the standpoint of a realignment of Christian ethics that can only be found in the context of the church. Thus, his theology of conflict resolution is based on a correct understanding of ecclesiology. Church fights and disagreements between individuals and the organization can become beneficial when the sources of the conflicts are identified and the people involved become respectful of each other and are assertive in their determination to work for the common good of the broader community. According to Halverstadt, the conflict manager must understand his own "gut theology" and begin to understand whether he is a part of the conflict or simply a bystander. Halverstadt graphs steps to resolving conflict from initially identifying perceived tension through a process that appraises conflict and then focuses on bringing it to a positive conclusion.[1]

Chris Argyris, in *Intervention Theory and Method: A Behavioral Science View*, developed three major steps vital to effective conflict intervention:

1. Generate valid and useful information. This separates truth from error; it explores the assumptions and interests of the different conflict parties and purges rumors and charges.

[1]Hugh F. Halverstadt, *Managing Church Conflict*, (Louisville, KY: Westminster/John Knox Press, 1991), 4, 15–24.

2. Allow free and informed choice. Conflict parties must feel safe enough for honesty about their own feelings concerning the conflict issues and relationships.

3. Motivate internal commitment to the plan or agreements reached. This means that the choice of action has been internalized by each member so that each person experiences a high degree of ownership and commitment and accepts responsibility for the choice and its implications.[2]

Argyris also says that when leaders are involved in conflict resolution, their primary leadership skills involve reflective listening, empathic understanding, care giving, and discernment. The parties involved in the conflict must believe the process is fair, that they will get a fair hearing, and that they will have an opportunity to influence the outcomes.[3]

Roger Heuser details methods of dealing with conflict in "Conflict Intervention Overview" that are applicable when teaching conflict management to missionaries in the Asia Pacific region, which is the focus of this project. Heuser provides models of intervention and tools that can be used to help address the situations cross-culturally.[4]

Dean Anderson and Linda Anderson, in the book Beyond *Change Management: Advanced Strategies for Today's Transformational Leaders*, look at various stages of consciousness and competence in order to understand the source of conflict and how it can be alleviated.

1. Unconscious incompetence is the initial stage that individuals develop through an inability to deal with changes, inconveniences, or things they do not understand.

2. Conscious incompetence follows as people struggle to deal with situations without an understanding of how to deal with the issues.

3. Conscious competence is where people learn to grapple with the problems and acquire knowledge on conflict resolution.

4. Finally, unconscious competence develops in the parties involved.[5]

The information from this book can be used to assess and clarify the needs for growing awareness and skills for effective conflict resolution and is helpful as this project develops training processes for new and veteran missionaries in the area of change.

---

[2] Chris Argyris, *Intervention Theory and Method: A Behavioral Science View*, (Reading, MA: Addison-Wesley, 1970), 19–25.
[3] Ibid., 15–16.
[4] Roger Heuser, "Conflict Intervention Overview"(paper presented during Managing Conflict and Change class at Asia Pacific Theological Seminary, Baguio, Philippines, on 10 February, 2007).
[5] Dean Anderson and Linda Anderson, *Beyond Change Management: Advanced Strategies for Today's Transformational Leaders*, (San Francisco: Jossey-Bass Publishers, 2001), 136–147.

Cross-Cultural Conflict and Missionary Longevity

The project will engage conflict between missionaries and the national church in its teaching processes. Jerry W. Robinson, Jr. and Roy A. Clifford, in *Conflict Management in Community Groups*, analyze cross-cultural conflict. They focus on several stages through which tension builds to conflict. Conflict is approached from the standpoint of developing responses through the community's involvement. Their book informs the process through which tension develops and identifies reasons that can be dealt with by community groups. The initial stage of conflict resolution is tension development that emphasizes communication.[6]

Duane Elmer, in *Cross Cultural Conflict: Building Relationships for Effective Ministry*, gives theological reasons why conflicts can be alleviated by the intervention of people who are committed to working in other cultures. He speaks of all people having the image of God and says that love must be culturally defined. However, there are also many diverse cultures and views within the U.S. Often family background and dynamics have significant impact on relationships on the field. Family interaction and background issues can often add to confusion and the stress individuals experience while living in another culture. Elmer identifies five conflict strategies that work in the Western World and in the Majority World. These strategies can be used in the project to train missionaries during the annual missionary renewal sessions allotted to the Asia Pacific staff.

1. The win-lose strategy. This adheres to the belief that there is a right and wrong position with little in between. These individuals believe there is only one right answer for most situations. The tactics this person uses include physical force, threats, intimidation, silence, volume of verbiage, and other manipulative tactics. These individuals are competitive and are often willing to sacrifice relationships to win. It is difficult for them to let go of any problem they do not see resolved in their favor.

2. Conflict avoidance. Some believe that all conflict is wrong so they avoid it at all costs. Unfortunately, these individuals have difficulty maintaining their goals and values as well as often losing their influence and even relationships.

3. Giving in. Some give in to accommodate those who oppose them. When the issues are not critical, giving in can eliminate unnecessary conflict;

---

[6] Jerry W. Robinson, Jr. and Roy A. Clifford, "Conflict Management in Community Groups," North-*Central Regional Extension Publication* No. 36–5, (Urbana, IL: University of Illinois at Urbana-Champaign, 1974).

however, when people give in just to appease others, there can be a loss of integrity.

4. Compromise. This can cause difficulties in some situations. Compromise is not necessarily bad in every case, and it can help bring resolution if there is a serious conflict.

5. Carefronting. The best way to handle conflict is what Elmer calls "Carefronting," which is designed to create a win-win situation. This approach includes: (a) the two parties come together, meet face to face, and talk openly and honestly. (b) They each make a commitment to preserve the relationship and dispassionately explain the values/goals that each wishes to protect or achieve. (c) They can creatively find a solution in which they can both be equal winners, with neither giving up anything of value, thus preserving the relationship. (d) They can do this with reason, keeping emotions under control. (e) They are both able to separate the person from the issues and speak objectively to that end. (f) Neither is satisfied with a solution until the other is also completely at peace with it.[7]

Carefronting, as a method of addressing conflict is practical and biblical. It is difficult to either understand the questions others have or find common ground toward a solution without talking together and trying to understand each one's perspective.

Roxane Lulofs describes several possible responses to conflict in *Conflict: From Theory to Action:* (1) Change the behavior of others or one's own behavior in the conflict. However, it is often difficult if not impossible to change the behavior of others if they do not see the need for change or do not want to change. Changing one's own behavior and attitudes is far easier than changing that of another person. (2) Changing the structure of the conflict means a change in the conditions that give rise to it; this includes increasing resources, changing the way resources are distributed, changing the nature of an interdependent relationship, changing goals, etc. This option is possible if the full array of information about a problem has been previously unexamined. In the course of exploring various options in a conflict, the structure of the conflict may be changed, or one can change oneself.[8]

---

[7] Duane Elmer, *Cross Cultural Conflict: Building Relationships for Effective Ministry*, (Downers Grove, IL: InterVarsity Press, 1993), 13, 35–43.

[8] Roxane S. Lulofs, *Conflicts: From Theory to Action*, (Scottsdale, AZ: Gorsuch Scarisbrick Publishers, 1994), 198.

Lulofs defines "conflict pollutants" as obstacles to conflict resolutions that complicate the issues and make resolution difficult. They are often ancillary elements that distract from the actual issues and interfere with peace-making.[9]

1. Preferences above principles. Conflict occurs over style-oriented options rather than imperatives. Preferences and nuisances are one type of conflict. When preference issues are added to central problems and distract attention from the more important issues, they become a pollutant.

2. Overblown expectations or expecting too much change too quickly. This can create a climate for failure and become an issue itself. Poor feedback skills are also a pollutant in conflicts when people confuse the conflict issue with the person.

3. Other pollutants include negativism and joylessness or overblown expectations. There can be many other pollutants, and if they are identified and effort given to remove them, most situations have a much greater possibility for a good and acceptable resolution.[10]

For resolution in conflicts, there must be an atmosphere of cooperation and not competition. When conflict occurs it is important to focus on cooperation in finding the best solution. Lulofs defines a cooperative climate as one that involves honest communication of relevant items that are involved in the conflict. A competitive atmosphere hinders resolution. An atmosphere of cooperation reduces tension and mistrust and increases the willingness of those involved to respond to each other's needs. There is an increased sensitivity to similarities and common interests rather than a focus on differences and threats. When the processes are cooperative rather than competitive, conflict becomes a matter of mutuality, a problem that is solved rather than a win-lose situation.[11]

In his book *The DNA of Relationships*, Gary Smalley refers to a "no-loser policy" when we all see ourselves on the same team. When this occurs there will not be a winner and loser because either both win or both lose. How does this impact a situation where there is conflict? Those involved keep talking until all come to a level of satisfaction where they have been heard, understood, and given adequate consideration. Even if only one person is committed to a no-loser policy, it can still make a significant difference in the outcome. Such a commitment goes a long way toward creating the kind of relationships that produce joy and satisfaction rather

---

[9] Ibid., 196–198.
[10] Lulofs, 203.
[11] Ibid., 196–205.

than frustration and grief. Winning becomes finding a solution that all can feel good about.[12] This concept is an important contribution to the project's training focus on cross-cultural conflict management.

Rick Brinkman and Rick Kirscher, in *Dealing with People You Can't Stand: How to Bring Out the Best in People at Their Worst*, indicate that every behavior has a purpose or intent that is fulfilled. People engage in behaviors based on their intent and do what they do based on what seems most important in any given moment. The focus is either on the task or on people. That focus is either aggressive or passive regardless of the goal. A person can focus on people aggressively, even belligerently. They can be assertive and involved or passive and submissive. They can focus on a task with aggression and with bold determination, or assertively with involvement, or passively and withdraw. Brinkman and Kirscher describe the four intents as: (1) get the task done; (2) get the task right; (3) get along with people; and (4) get appreciation from people.

Brinkman and Kirschner believe that each of these intents have their proper place, and when they are in balance it will reduce stress and conflict and result in greater success. If any of the intents are out of bounds or undue stress is present, it can and usually will produce conflict. When we begin a project, the goal is to complete it and have it done correctly. This will help eliminate unnecessary or repeated effort. When a team is involved, it is important that everyone is on board and supports the project. If they are to succeed, there must be ownership and affirmation given for a job well done. People need to believe that their effort is making a difference and is appreciated by those around them. One disgruntled person with the ability to disrupt the work of everyone around them makes for an interesting dynamic.[13] The four intentions contribute an understanding of conflict resolution that is of value to the teaching on conflict resolution in the project's training emphasis in pre-field training of new missionaries and during the regional studies sessions when new and veteran missionaries are present.

Conflict Resolution

A third component of managing conflict involves conflict within the national church. The project will engage this through instruction and through the mentoring process. Jesus gave special honor to peacemakers when he placed them among the beatitudes: "Blessed are the peacemakers, for they shall be called the sons/daughters

---

[12] Gary Smalley, *The DNA of Relationships*, (Wheaton, Illinois: Tyndale Publishers, 2004), 155–65.

[13] Rick Brinkman and Rick Kirschner, *Dealing With People You Can't Stand: How to Bring Out the Best in People at Their Worst*, (New York, NY: McGraw-Hill Publisher, 2002), 14–20

of God" (Matt. 5:9). Those who help bring reconciliation are a calming influence, and those who help bring peace to those in conflict are honored as God's children.

The origin of conflict is found in the sinful nature of man that followed a broken relationship between the first couple, Adam and Eve, and the Lord (Genesis 3). That sinful nature continued in their children when Cain killed his brother, Abel (Genesis 4). In both the Old and New Testaments we read of various situations where conflict occurred. In Genesis 27, we see it between Jacob and Esau; in Genesis 37, it is between Joseph and his brothers; in 1 Samuel, it is between Saul and David; in Mark 9:38, it is among the disciples; and in 1 Corinthians, we see it among groups in the church.

Mark Thiessen Nation, in *"Toward a Theology for Conflict Transformation: Learnings from John Howard Yoder,"* relates that conflict is a part of humanity's relationship struggles. Because of this, there is the need for a theology of conflict management. In order to accomplish this, Nation analyzes the Mennonite pacifist approach of John Howard Yoder because Nation believes that Yoder captures the essence of a Christian peacemaker in times of conflict. Nation identifies four elements crucial to managing conflict and being a peacemaker.

1. The centrality of Jesus. The centrality of Christ is the core around which peacemaking is constructed. Because God, as revealed through Jesus, is the center and not human reasoning, humility is formed that informs how we relate to others and strengthens our desire for justice and peace.

2. The Christian community. Skills are required for peacemaking, but at its core peacemaking is a "way of life." As Christians worship Jesus, they form a community that shares a common bond through worship. There are six personal qualities endemic to the peacemaking ability of the Christian community: (a) vulnerability that shows a willingness for both sides to admit that they misunderstand the others; (b) a willingness "not to get the credit"; (c) the ability for consistency in a long-term commitment to success; (d) to develop a network of compassionate believers in whom you can trust and who offer encouragement and valid critique; (e) a commitment to the other party's dignity; and (f) an understanding that through God each person has different giftings.[14]

3. The church must be the church. An understanding that there is a distinction between the church and the world is crucial for "conflict

---

[14] Ibid., 54–55.

transformation." The Christian's identity and allegiance is found in the church. Nation quotes Yoder, writing, "the church's responsibility to and for the world is first and always to be the church."[15]

4.   The church must understand the nature of sin. If we do not have a vocabulary that describes sin, then we fall short in attempting to deal with wrongs or evil. Nation cites Long's statement about understanding the nature of sin by the vocabulary used to describe it: "One can only think of Jesus' crucifixion as 'an unfortunate but avoidable failure in communication' if one believes that the remedy for sin is merely better training in the techniques of conflict resolution."[16]

Ken Sande, in *The Peacemaker: A Biblical Guide to Resolving Personal Conflict*, provides excellent Biblical values and practical information on bringing positive solutions during times of conflict. He identifies three basic ways that people respond to conflict. They will try to escape from conflict, attack others during conflict, or respond with peacemaking. When people are more interested in avoiding conflict than in resolving it, they will try to escape. One way they try to escape is through denial. They either deny that conflict exists, or they bypass it and make no attempt to address the situation. They may also attempt to run away from conflict by relocating to another place either temporarily or permanently. We see the prodigal son in Luke 15 leaving because he did not like the restrictions of living at home.

Sande says the "attack response" is used by people who are more interested in winning a conflict than in preserving a relationship. If conflict is seen as a contest, an opportunity of exerting one's rights, to control others or take advantage of a situation, then the attack response might be applied. This response is often used by people who are strong or self-confident. It might also be used by someone who feels cornered and thinks his only option is to lash out due to fear or insecurity. This may include verbal attacks, violence, or even litigation. For Christians this response will damage their witness to the community and those around them. In 1 Corinthians 6:1–8, Paul cautions Christians about going to court, and encourages them to settle their differences within the church.

Sande indicates that the "peacemaking response" includes several approaches to conflict with the goal of bringing peace to that situation. If a dispute is really insignificant it is overlooked. This is simply forgiving and releasing the person by

---

[15] Ibid., 56.

[16] Mark Thiessen Nation, "Toward a Theology for Conflict Transformation: Learnings from John Howard Yoder," in *The Mennonite Quarterly Review*, 80, 1, January 2006, 43–57.

making no effort to retaliate or holding a grudge. It might involve reconciliation by going to the person and resolving the issue just between the two alone. Matthew 5:23 says this should be done before a gift is given to the Lord so it will be acceptable. If the situation cannot be resolved between the two, then mediation is needed. Others become involved as Jesus mentions in Matthew 18:16. It might include arbitration within the church as Paul suggests in 1 Corinthians 6, and it allows people's accountability to Christian leaders. James 3:18 emphasizes an important result in reminding us that "peacemakers who sow in peace, raise a harvest of righteousness." When other Christians are involved, they can help bring restoration and healing, thereby helping to save the relationship from division as justice and peace are administered.

Sande makes an interesting observation that those who try to escape are usually focused on "me." Their priority is themselves, and they are looking for what is convenient, easy, or not threatening. When someone uses the attack response, his focus is on "you," blaming you and expecting you to give in and solve the problem. In the peacemaking response, the focus is on "us." All are given consideration and there is a mutual responsibility to solve the problem. The author calls escaping "peace-faking" as they try to make the situation look better than it really is. He calls the attack response "peace-breaking" when someone is willing to sacrifice anything to get what he wants. The right approach is "peacemaking" which results in harmony with others as well as justice.[17]

Joshua N. Weiss, in *You Didn't Just Say That: Quotes, Quips, and Proverbs For Dealing In The World of Conflict And Negotiation*, indicates that conflict produces hurtful results for people and for organizations, such as anger, broken relationships, pain, anguish, stress, and frustration. However, he asserts that it does not have to always be negative because conflict can be beneficial if people have the skills to manage it successfully. Conflict, correctly led and mediated, can lead to positive outcomes and results.[18]

Edwin H. Friedman indicates in *A Failure of Nerve: Leadership in the Age of the Quick Fix* that it is important that those involved in conflict resolution not give up but keep trying. He enumerates ten suggestions that are beneficial to this project preparing missionaries to handle conflict through pre-field, missionary renewal

---

[17] Ken Sande, *The Peacemaker: A Biblical Guide to Resolving Personal Conflict*, (Grand Rapids, Michigan: Baker Books, 2004), 21–30.

[18] Joshua N. Weiss, *You Didn't Just Say That: Quotes, Quips, and Proverbs For Dealing In The World of Conflict And Negotiation*, (Cambridge, MA: Program on Negotiation, Harvard Law School, 2005), available from <http://www.pon.org/downloads/quote_book.pdf>, accessed 20 March 2007

sessions, and on-field counseling and training in an attempt to help people be successful in conflict resolution.

1. Keep functioning. Do not let a crisis become the axis around which your whole world revolves.

2. Develop a support system outside of work. Find people who can help you with the issues such as professionals in the field of conflict management, and people who can help shoulder the load such as family members and trusted friends.

3. Stay focused on long-term goals. Do not allow the day-to-day problems that arise deter you from goals that take time to mature. Conflicts should also not dissuade you from the importance of your long-term goals.

4. Deep breathing, prayer or meditation. Make sure to schedule alone times where you can meditate and commune with God.

5. Listen to your body. Don't allow the work load or the stress of dealing with a crisis overload you.

6. Watch the emotional triangles (Friedman, 209–226). Emotional triangles form when two entities engage with a third. Friedman's "emotional triangles explain how people are drawn into conflict with two other parties. This can happen when two people in a church, business, or family interact with a third person, such as a pastor, missionary, or business partner. Little good happens when a leader become enmeshed in these emotional triangles except broken relationships. The best a person can do is to establish and maintain individual relationships with each party without getting between two persons that are in some type of conflict.

7. Work out the balance between being responsible for self and being labeled unfriendly or aggressive.

8. In relationships, keep anxiety in check with an infusion of humor (Friedman, 242).

9. When the same questions bring no new information, it is time to make decisions. Do not let things become a drag on the system. Do not let things start to drag out and create stress from indeciveness.

10. Accept the possibility that one's own attitudes and actions brought on the conflict. If issues stem from your own actions, you may be able to influence restoration yourself.[19]

---

[19] Edwin H. Friedman, *A Failure of Nerve: Leadership in the Age of the Quick Fix*, (Bethesda, MD: The Edwin Friedman Estate/Trust, 1999), 302–15.

The mission organization can effectively assist the field missionary in the areas of mentoring, coaching and conflict management. A mentoring program between new personnel and selected veteran missionaries on the field in Asia Pacific is already in place. This can be augmented to become a more in-depth program. New missionary training needs to include cross-cultural conflict resolution between missionaries and also between missionaries and the national church including steps for becoming peacemakers on the field.

Biblical Models for Longevity

The biblical narrative portrays God in the Old Testament and Christ and the apostles in the New Testament as concerned about the ability of their followers to finish their spiritual journey well. This section will examine how the Old Testament portrays God's concern for finishing well and the New Testament's revelation of Christ's concern and the subsequent teaching of the apostles about finishing well.

The Old Testament and Longevity

This section will look at the Old Testament foundation of God's attitude towards humanity's ability to persevere and to finish what he calls them to do. Throughout the Old Testament there is evidence that God wants people to finish well. God says in Scripture, "Even to your old age and gray hairs I am he, I am he who will sustain you. I have made you and I will carry you; I will sustain you and I will rescue you" (Isaiah 46:4). In the Garden of Eden there is evidence of God preparing pre-fallen Adam and Eve's success. This is God's loving and nurturing nature revealed in his dealings with humanity.

David Atkinson, in *The Message of Genesis 1–11: The Dawn of Creation*, looks at the theological message that comes from the creation and relates that in the second chapter of Genesis a Creator God is observed who loved and nurtured humanity.Atkinson describes him as concerned for all aspects of humanity's existence and success. Atkinson's premise is that God acts as a "near, fatherly, covenant God, *Yahweh Elohim*" on behalf of his people and is concerned with anything that hinders their successful service to him.[20] This is an important message to present in the training of new missionaries and to reiterate to veterans.

Dietrich Bonhoeffer, in *Creation and fall: A Theological Exposition of Genesis 1–3*, relates a message that God deals with people who are plagued with trouble in a nurturing and caring manner. The idea is that this caring and nurturing God is

---

[20]David Atkinson, *The Message of Genesis 1–11: The Dawn of Creation*, (Downers Grove, IL: InterVarsity Press, 1990), 55.

concerned that his people be successful in their service and worship of him to the end of their lives. Bonhoeffer indicates that even in the restrictions about the Tree of Knowledge that God placed in the garden, he was preparing Adam to make choices that helped him become a moral person and that by obeying God's instructions concerning the forbidden fruit, Adam learned faithfulness and obedience—vital elements in finishing well.[21] God taught Adam and Eve *analogia relationis* ("analogy of relationship"), which meant that by drawing near to God a relationship developed, enabling the first couple to finish their commission well. However, because of their disobedience they did not finish well in the Garden, which opened the door to moral failure and the resulting shame.[22]

God made it possible for people to finish well by attempting to develop and shape their character. Paul House, in *Old Testament Theology*, states that in biblical history God dealt harshly with the nations for ignoring him (cf. Isa. 13–23; Jer. 46–51; Ezek. 1–32; Amos 1–2). God's judgment was always associated with his willingness to forgive those who repented. This is evidence of his attempt at refining and purifying them so they might inherit the kingdom of God (cf. Isa. 11:1–10; 65–66; Jer. 31–32; Ezek. 33–48; Zeph. 3:8–20). In so doing, God was teaching all nations, including Israel, the qualities of humility, submission, and repentance, qualities necessary to go through life successfully.[23]

In The Knowledge of the Holy: *The Attributes of God: Their Meaning in the Christian Life*, A. W. Tozer relates how God's faithfulness, goodness, mercy, grace, and love shape our understanding of him. As our understanding of him and his nature grows, we learn the eternal virtues that enable us to live successful lives in relationship with God and with other people. We learn that his faithfulness, which is based upon his goodness, is what our hope of salvation rests upon. Tozer discusses the holistic nature of God's character as revealed in his goodness in addressing human guilt through mercy, while grace "imputes merit" to individuals. Added to his mercy and grace, God's justice expresses the idea of "moral equity," which is the opposite of the inequality that comes through iniquity. His judgment is the application of equity and teaches humanity the nature of equality that is found in his justice. For believers, this is applicable to everyday life in ministry, especially in situations where conflicts arise from inequities.[24]

---

[21] Dietrich Bonhoeffer, *Creation and Fall: A Theological Exposition of Genesis 1–3*, ed. John W. de Gruchy, trans. Douglas Stephen Bax (Minneapolis, MN: Fortress Press, 1997), 103.

[22] Bonhoeffer, *Creation and Fall*, 103.

[23] Paul R. House, *Old Testament Theology* (Downers Grove, IL: InterVarsity Press, 1998), 542.

[24] A. W. Tozer, *The Knowledge of the Holy: The Attributes of God: Their Meaning in the Christian Life*, (New York: Harper & Row, 1961), 88, 93, 100, 106–07, 109.

Millard J. Erickson, in God the Father Almighty: A Contemporary Exploration of the Divine Attributes, agrees that God attempts to shape people's character in ways that produces fruit of longevity throughout the Bible. God is longsuffering and, even when people make mistakes and repent, he is willing to reconcile with them and help them reestablish themselves so that they might finish well.[25]

The Law, God's Covenants, and Longevity

Colin G. Kruse's article, "Law," in the New Dictionary of Biblical Theology, shows that the development of the Old Testament Law was an attempt to lead Israel to a successful walk before God. The books of Joshua through 2 Kings taught Israel the holistic blessing of obedience and the bitter failure of disobedience. Further, the prophets showed Israel how to correct wrong actions and attitudes and how to gain restoration each time they fell. Kruse describes how Amos, Hosea, Jeremiah, Daniel, Ezra, and Nehemiah (the latter prophets) delivered the message that disobeying God created damaged relationships with God, disunity with others in the community, and ultimately leads to moral failure which keeps people from finishing well. The good news is that restoration is also built into the Law, which reveals God's concern for people to finish well and is an underlying concept behind the Law and redemption.[26]

Stephen Westerholm, in Perspectives Old and New on Paul: The "Lutheran" Paul and His Critics, discusses how the "Lutheran Paul" thought the Law revealed God's concern for all aspects of humanity. This includes how Israel relates to God in worship and obedience, to themselves as people of integrity, and to others by justice shown to the weak, the fatherless, and strangers. Paul understood that the Law addresses the human condition in a positive manner as it shows men and women how to live, work, and coexist with each other, living with integrity throughout their lives. In essence, Paul believed that God shows humanity how to finish well through the truths that are revealed in the Law. So, to Paul, the Law's purpose was to produce a moral person who obeyed and worshipped God and lived in peace with others. This is observed in the Ten Commandments (Exod. 20:1–17) where the first four commandments relate to humanity's relationship with God and the last six deal with relating to others. The holistic nature of Paul's Old Testament God was revealed in

---

[25] Millard J. Erickson, God the Father Almighty: A Contemporary Exploration of the Divine Attributes (Grand Rapids, MI: Baker Books, 1998), 233–4.

[26] Colin G. Kruse, "Law," in New Dictionary of Biblical Theology, ed. T. Desmond Alexander, Brian S. Rosner, D. A. Carson, and Graeme Goldsworthy (Downers Grove, IL: InterVarsity Press, 2000), 631–633.

God's formalized instructions of how to worship him, how to gain forgiveness of sin, and how to relate to one another and to strangers.[27]

Paul R. Williamson's chapter, "Covenant," in *The New Dictionary of Biblical Theology*, describes how God's covenants seal relationships between himself and his people. God does this by binding himself to promises that include reciprocal responses from the people. In so doing, God enables people to successfully follow him and be fruitful in their lives. For people to fail in fulfilling the covenantal requirements, failure is guaranteed. This indicates that maintaining a covenantal relationship with God enables believers to finish their lives well. God intends for his people's success as they follow him, but humanity's self-will often leads to their downfall. Williamson's understanding of the book of Hebrews views Christ as the incarnate covenantal promise that supersedes all previous covenants (Heb. 7:22; 8:6 to 10:31; 12:18–24; 13:20). Under the new covenant through Jesus, the Holy Spirit is the one who enables believers who are faithful to Christ to overcome through him (Heb. 8:10–12; 10:16–17).[28] This enables believers to live victoriously in spite of their circumstance, and to finish their lives successfully in Christ.

Bill Mills and Craig Parro, in *Finishing Well in Life and Ministry: God's Protection from Burnout*, identify essential elements found in Jesus' life that contribute to finishing well. They use the examples of three people in the Old Testament who finished well in spite of difficult circumstances to shed light on those qualities found in Jesus. The three Old Testament figures are:

1. Elijah. He felt alone and overwhelmed in his dealings with Ahab and Jezebel, yet God protected him, provided sleep for him in his exhaustion, gave him food, water, and shelter, answered Elijah's hard questions, and provided him with a ministry partner—Elisha. The key to Elijah's finishing well was his commitment to stand in God's presence (1 Kings 19:11).

2. Moses. He led God's people out of Egyptian servitude and gave God's Law, but he felt inadequate to the task. Finishing well for Moses was his discovery that without God's presence he was incapable of going on (Exod. 33:12–16).

3. David. He was not perfect and failed morally on different occasions. However, his tender heart towards God and his thirst for God's presence

---

[27] Stephen Westerholm, *Perspectives Old and New on Paul: The "Lutheran" Paul and His Critics* (Grand Rapids, MI: Eerdmans, 2004), 321, 334–35.

[28] Paul R. Williamson, "Covenant," in *New Dictionary of Biblical Theology*, ed. T. Desmond Alexander, Brian S. Rosner, D. A. Carson, and Graeme Goldsworthy (Downers Grove, IL: InterVarsity Press, 2000), 423–29.

led him to repent of his sins and turn back to God. Even though David had some serious lapses, in the end he finished well.[29]

Mills and Parro highlight the ability of Jesus to overcome temptations and burnout as he entered the hectic spotlight of his ministry and was able to finish well. He suffered pressures because: (1) his life was in danger (Luke 4:29; John 7:1); (2) he had a hectic schedule and constantly needed to take time for prayer in order to receive refreshing (Matt. 26:37–39; Luke 22:43–44); and (3) he was tempted as any human is tempted. Immediately after his baptism he was led by the Spirit into the wilderness for forty days. At the end he endured a series of temptations that were targeted specifically to his divinity and his sense of God's purpose in his life (Luke 3:21–22; 4:1–3, 5–7, 9–11).[30]

Mills and Parro identify keys to Jesus' ability to overcome the stresses and temptations so he could successfully finish his life's work with his integrity intact in his surrender to his Father's will.

1. He rested in the assurance that he was accepted and loved by his Father (Luke 3:21–22; John 2:24–25) and that he worked according to his Father's timetable (John 7:6) and agenda (John 7:18).
2. He avoided burnout by following his Father's lead in everything he did because God was the initiator of Christ's ministry (John 5:19–20, 30).
3. Jesus was a visionary, but his vision did not consume him or drive him to the point of burnout because the vision originated with God. He found peace as he pursued God's vision and found security in knowing that God was leading the way. This is how Jesus was able to finish well.[31]

Mills and Parro identify four elements from Jesus' example: (1) humility; (2) a servant's heart that is revealed through intimate relationships with others; (3) a commitment to the proclamation of an undiluted message of repentance and faith; and (4) manifest obedience to God's grace by being a faithful watchman over our own hearts and God's flock. Mills and Parro base Paul's ability to finish well in living a life that contained the "fullness of Christ."[32]

Mills and Parro consider Paul's theology had a highly developed understanding of Jesus as he related to the saved individual. Paul saw Christ as the visible image of God, the "firstborn over all creation," the source of all that exists, the creator of all

---

[29] Bill Mills and Craig Parro, *Finishing Well in Life and Ministry: God's Protection from Burnout* (Palos Heights, IL: Leadership Resources International, 1998), 32–35.
[30] Ibid., 131–135.
[31] Ibid., 145–150.
[32] Ibid., 225–35.

things, and the substance that holds all things together (Col. 1:15–17; 2:9–10). Paul's view of the fullness of God in Christ was his model for humanity's life in Christ. Paul labored in the energy of Christ who resided in him (Col. 1:29).[33]

The New Testament and Longevity

A competent understanding of what successful completion of God-called ministry means is crucial to the development of missionary retention processes developed in this research. The New Testament chronicles God's successful redemption of humanity through his son Jesus Christ and the establishment of God's Kingdom on the earth.

Finishing well is a consistent theme in the New Testament. Jesus consistently shows his concern for his followers to finish well in their walk with him. In the Gospels, discipleship reflects the appropriate response to Christ's message. It indicates a change that causes a person to turn and begin following Christ. Michael J. Wilkins's *The Concept of Disciple in Matthew's Gospel: As Reflected in the Use of the Term Mathétés* says the term "discipleship" *(mathétés)* is used throughout the Gospels to reflect this new direction that is contained in Christ's teachings. Wilkins says the verb form, "make disciples" *(matheteuein)*, occurs only three times in Matthew (13:52; 27:57; 28:19) and once in Acts (14:21). Its appearance in Matthew 28:19 is its only usage in an imperative form. In the pre-Christ era the term reflected those who were students of a particular teacher. In this usage Wilkins indicates the students chose the teacher they followed and the teacher taught about different wisdom aspects of life or politics. The students followed the teacher until they had sufficient knowledge and ability to attract followers of their own and begin their own "master/student" relationships.[34]

David J. Bosch's *Transforming Mission: Paradigm Shifts in Theology of Mission* agrees that Jesus' purpose for his followers is reflected in how he changed the "master/disciple" relationship. Jesus chose them, they did not choose him. They were called to follow. Jesus' teaching was not about esoteric philosophies of life or politics but about the kingdom of God and how humanity related to it and about himself. Jesus' followers were never to branch out into their own "master/disciples" relationships but were Christ's disciples continually and were his servants continually. Jesus' followers were not trained "teachers" but were "witnesses" of the

---

[33]Ibid., 251–71.

[34] Michael J. Wilkins, *The Concept of Disciple in Matthew's Gospel: As Reflected in the Use of the Term mathétés* (New York,: E. J. Brill, 1988), 104–10; 128.

Kingdom, and they were at the eschatological forefront of God's kingdom. Bosch indicates that the noun form of "disciple" (mathētēs) is found numerous times in the gospels and the book of Acts—it never occurs in the epistles or Revelation. In the Gospels it is the only term used to describe followers of Jesus and occurs seventy-three times in Matthew, forty-six in Mark, thirty-seven in Luke, seventy-eight in John, and twenty-eight in Acts.[35]

Ronald J. Sider, in *Good News and Good Works: A Theology for the Whole Gospel*, indicates that the core of Jesus' teaching on discipleship was total, lifelong, unconditional submission to him as Master. Jesus was concerned that his disciples understand the nature of the commitment required to follow him (Matt. 8:18–22; Luke 9:57–62). His followers were to follow him based upon careful consideration (Luke 14:25–35) and a commitment to give up their lives in his service (Matt. 16:24 –26; Mark 8:34–36; Luke 9:23–26).[36]

J. B. Hixson, in *Making Disciples: Rethinking the Church's Mission: A Comparison and Contrast of Discipleship Concepts in the Synoptic Gospels and Discipleship Concepts in the Epistles*, says that the apostles reflected Christ's concern for finishing well in their teaching about following Christ. After the Gospels, the use of the term mathētēs for discipleship begins to fade and is not used in the Epistles but is replaced by the active terms "walk" and "follow." "Walk" is used twenty-one times in the Synoptic Gospels and eight times in Acts to refer to the actual physical act of walking, while in the Epistles each of the forty-one times it occurs it refers to behavior, specifically the behavior of those who follow Christ.[37] Hixson says that the apostles Paul and John understood that walking in the Lord indicated a growth and maturity that enabled them to behave as representatives of God's kingdom. The emphasis on right behavior indicates a concern for not only beginning to follow Jesus at conversion but a continuous lifestyle of submission and servitude to Christ that takes them to the end of their spiritual journey. This indicates a desire on the apostles' part of both beginning and continuing a walk in Christ until the end. Finishing well is implied.

The emphasis on finishing well was communicated in Paul's writings and should be included in the project's biblical design to train missionaries. As Paul said, "so that I may finish my race with joy, and the ministry which I received from the

---

[35] David J. Bosch, *Transforming Mission: Paradigm Shifts in Theology of Mission* (Maryknoll, NY: Orbis Books, 1991), 37–39, 73.

[36] Ronald J. Sider, *Good News and Good Works: A Theology for the Whole Gospel* (Grand Rapids, MI: Baker Books, 1993), 110.

[37] J. B. Hixson, "Making Disciples: Rethinking the Church's Mission: A Comparison and Contrast of Discipleship Concepts in the Synoptic Gospels and Discipleship Concepts in the Epistles," *Global Ed Net*, http://www.globalednet.org/gen/papers/papers.asp, accessed, April 18, 2010: 13.

Lord Jesus, to testify to the gospel of the grace of God" (Acts 20:24b). Jeffrey A. D. Weima, in *How You Must Walk to Please God: Holiness and Discipleship in 1 Thessalonians,* says that in 1 Thessalonians, Paul expresses a concern for living holy lives in order to please God (1 Thess. 3:13). In 4:1–12, Paul specifically deals with idleness and sexual immorality by calling upon followers of Christ to live "holy" lives. The eventual end of the life of a follower of Jesus is affected by how he deals with the temptation to sexual unfaithfulness and also his view of work. Both will affect how the follower of Christ ends his or her life and ministry.[38]

Gerald F. Hawthorne, in *The Imitation of Christ: Discipleship in Philippians,* reveals that Paul was concerned about being an example, which is an important principle to include in missionary training instruction on mentoring younger missionaries. In 1 Corinthians, he says specifically, "Therefore I urge you to imitate me" (1 Cor. 4:16). Paul expresses this five times in the New Testament (1 Cor. 4:16; 11:1; Phil. 3:17; 2 Thess. 3:7, 9; cf. Gal. 4:12; Phil. 4:9). Paul's use of imitation has its roots in Paul's imitation of Christ, "Follow my example, as I follow the example of Christ" (1 Cor. 11:1). The imitation (imitatio) of Christ has a normative character as the person consciously attempts Christlikeness. In Paul's defense of himself in 1 Corinthians, he indicates that his life, which is modeled on Christ, is intertwined with his gospel. Hawthorne states that following Jesus is about a relationship with him that is not just cerebral but is lived out in everyday life. Beliefs (orthodoxy) are important, but so is practice (orthopraxis).[39]

Frank Thielman, in *The NIV Application Commentary: Philippians,* indicates that Paul was concerned with living a consistent life (Phil. 2:16) and he encouraged believers to "avoid the mistakes of the past, give up their discord, and present a unified witness to the dark world around them."[40] He was concerned with living a disciplined life (1 Cor. 9:26–27) so that he might be consistent to the end. He went to Jerusalem to consult with the council in Acts 15 because, as he explained in Galatians, "for fear that I was running or had run my race in vain" (Gal. 2:2). He exhorted followers to continually examine themselves so that they would not fall short in following Jesus by saying, "Examine yourselves to see whether you are in the faith; test yourselves. Do you not realize that Christ Jesus is in you—unless, of

---

[38] Jeffrey A. D. Weima, "'How You Must Walk to Please God': Holiness and Discipleship in 1 Thessalonians," in *Patterns of Discipleship in the New Testament,* ed. Richard N. Longenecker (Grand Rapids, MI: William B. Eerdmans, 1996), 98–99.

[39] Gerald F. Hawthorne, "The Imitation of Christ: Discipleship in Philippians," in *Patterns of Discipleship in the New Testament,* ed. Richard N. Longenecker (Grand Rapids, MI: William B. Eerdmans, 1996), 165–66.

[40] Frank Thielman, *The NIV Application Commentary: Philippians* (Grand Rapids, MI: Zondervan, 1995), 140.

course, you fail the test?" (2 Cor. 13:5). Being faithful to the end was important for Paul, and it is not accidental that he requested that Timothy pursue, among other things, endurance when he said, "But you, man of God, flee from all this, and pursue righteousness, godliness, faith, love, *endurance* and gentleness" (1 Tim. 6:11, emphasis added).

The biblical models for missionary longevity and finishing well included evidence from the Old Testament. Beginning in Genesis with Adam and Eve, God made it possible for people to finish well by attempting to develop and shape their character. The Old Testament Law attempted to lead Israel to a successful walk before God. The prophets showed Israel how to correct wrong actions and attitudes and be restored. God's covenants sealed relationships between God and his people. Elijah, Moses, and David discovered how to finish well. Jesus is the incarnate covenantal promise. Jesus overcame stresses and temptations to finish his life's work with integrity. Evidence from the New Testament for finishing well included discipleship which is the total, lifelong, unconditional submission to Christ as Master. The discipleship theme continued in Paul's writings in finishing well by imitating Christ in living a consistent life, faithful to the end.

Summary

Over the last three chapters I have sought to lay a foundation by describing why missionaries can leave the field too soon. To briefly recap, personal factors affecting missionary longevity included personal unhappiness, marriage, family problems which involved children's education as well as stresses in relocating the family to a new country. Physical and emotional health issues, culture shock and finances were also part of the personal factors that affected missionary longevity. Conflicts, poor administrative structures, dismissal and transfers to North American ministry were other issues involved as well. Data in the literature reviewed showed the effect unrealistic expectations had in missionary attrition. Factors affecting younger applicants stressed the role of student debt as well as the negative influences of web-based pornography. Lack of language learning, cultural adaptation, and teamwork were other issues mentioned. Younger applicants are more susceptible to distractions from the home front due to the instant availability of internet access. The sustaining factor of God's call and obedience to Christ along with spiritual formation stressed the importance of the missionary's commitment to the person of Christ and call of God that enables him or her to live a strong spiritual life and endure hardships.

Organizational factors impacting missionary longevity included the necessity of making retention a priority for the mission organization. Van Meter noted that the closer the mission-sending organization is to the church, the greater the retention rate.[41] It was noted that a mission organization needs to determine its own retention rate, determine missionary needs and develop an action plan to ensure missionary longevity. A mission organization is responsible to train leaders and include a process of accountability in the training process. Applicant screening, orientation, clear communication including job descriptions, developing a prayer culture, on-field training and handling evaluations, complaints, debriefings and contingency plans well are all important parts of an effective mission organization. Member care is a vital area that can help in reducing attrition. Member care can be seen in training relational skills for interpersonal conflict as well as training ministry skills and leadership development. Mentoring, coaching and conflict management training are valuable parts of the training process as well as providing personnel to serve as mentors, coaches and trainers. Evaluation is another important part of the mission organization. Self-assessment is important as well as having external evaluation.

Biblical/spiritual factors impacting missionary longevity included biblical models for longevity from both the Old Testament and the New Testament stressing finishing well. Discipleship and submission to Christ as Master, living a consistent life, and being faithful to the end was emphasized. With this foundation in mind, we now turn to evaluation of the field research.

----

[41]Van Meter, 26.

5 DESCRIPTION OF PROJECT RESEARCH METHODOLOGY

This chapter describes the project's intention to understand missionary attrition and longevity and the development of a process that will address the issues discovered in the research through the Asia Pacific Region training sessions, on-field workshops, counseling with missionaries, and at field and regional meetings.

The Design of the Project

This project evaluated attrition data gleaned from Assemblies of God World Missions personnel information to understand the rates of attrition over the past twenty-five years. The information is evaluated in five-year increments during that time to establish rates of attrition. Questionnaires were sent to veteran missionaries with more than one term of service in order to identify factors that contributed to their longevity. The information garnered through this research is the foundation for developing regional training and counseling programs that will address issues that have led to attrition and teaching sessions that will promote best practices for missionary longevity and finishing well.

The Scope of the Project

The scope of this project involves new missionaries, veteran missionaries, and retired missionaries. This information obtained will be used to develop training processes for candidate missionaries through the Asia Pacific Region's new missionary training program, which takes place each summer in Springfield, Missouri.

Surveys to veteran missionaries will identify positive elements for use as best practices in missionary life. This information will enable the region to develop on-going training during the annual Regional Studies sessions, which take place each summer in Springfield, Missouri. These meetings involve both new and veteran missionaries who are home to re-raise their support, which occurs at the end of each missionary's three or four year term.

Out of this project will also come on-going training during on-field meetings and retreats. These occur regularly and are times when missionaries come for rest and rejuvenation. These are opportunities to address issues that impact their ability to finish well.

This project will also serve as a source of information. It will inform area directors of attrition issues and longevity best practices as they interact with missionaries during field visits and counseling sessions. It will also provide information to the regions counseling ministry that addresses missionary issues. The information provided by this project will also serve to contribute to the broader understanding of missionary attrition and longevity.

The Context of the Project

This project is developed for use at new missionary candidate training sessions conducted in Springfield, Missouri prior to their commissioning as appointed missionaries and before they leave America. It will also be implemented for both candidate and veteran missionaries at the annual regional studies meetings conducted during the annual missionary renewal held in Springfield, Missouri. Further, this project will inform the counseling aspects of Asia Pacific Region's interaction with missionaries on the field.

The Major Phases of the Project

The project is carried out in four main phases. There is some overlapping of these phases, but they are carried out sequentially. They are accomplished over a period of approximately eighteen months.

Research Phase

During the research phase of this project, a review of pertinent literature about attrition and longevity of service was accomplished and presented in the previous chapters. Qualitative and quantitative research methods were then used to gather research information. The first method involved an analysis of Assemblies of God World Missions personnel records of missionaries who quit during a twenty-year time span (1986 to 2005). This research identified factors revealing why these missionaries left. These factors were coded into categories that were used to analyze the results. The second method of research involved a survey instrument with open-ended qualitative questions and Likert-scale quantitative questions. These were sent to veteran missionaries with more than one term of service. Analysis of the surveys attempted to understand the positive factors that contribute to missionary longevity, and to get veteran missionary input into reasons for attrition by asking them what almost made them quit.

The two areas of research, i.e., AGWM personnel records of missionary attrition from 1986-2005 and the survey instrument for veterans missionaries, form the basis of this dissertation field research. The literature review forms the foundation on which the field research is based. The results of these areas will then be used to develop the process that will address the issues discovered.

Planning Phase

In the planning phase of the project, each facet of the project was identified, with plans developed for implementation. The first step involved identifying literature and material that contributed to the successful completion of the project. Second, a careful study of the literature in the literature review chapter laid the foundation for the development of the project. Third, identifying, gathering, and analyzing personnel records produced an understanding of reasons for missionary attrition. Fourth, a survey instrument sent to veteran missionaries to identified best practices that contribute to missionary longevity and finishing well.

Another component of this project is the on-field implementation of instruction in missional best practices for finishing well during field visits, workshops, missionary retreats, and field conferences.

Action Phase

This project was implemented over a period of eighteen months as material was identified that informed the project about attrition and longevity. During this time, people proficient in the issues are identified and planning for the summer session is implemented.

Evaluation Phase

The evaluation phase of the project involved analyzing personnel records of departed missionaries and a thorough study of the survey instrument results. Both of these tasks identify attrition issues and longevity factors that were addressed during regional meetings. After careful analysis of the research and the training sessions, the final chapters of this project were written.

Contribution to Ministry

Information derived from this research assists future mission personnel in serving longer and more effectively in cross- cultural ministry. It can also assist in the selection process for new missionaries and the candidate orientation process to better prepare the organization and potential personnel.

This project will facilitate the design and implementation of a process within the Asia Pacific Region to adequately train missionary candidates before they go to the field during candidate training sessions and to emphasize positive best practices for returning veterans during regional studies at the annual Missionary Renewal in Springfield, Missouri. This project will inform regional counseling ministries of identified issues that cause attrition and information gleaned from veterans that contribute to longevity. The information gleaned from this project will also be used to develop on-going training during on-field meetings and retreats.

This project will assist regional and area directors as they deal with attritional issues that cause missionaries to become discouraged and want to resign. First, it will raise awareness of the negative issues that impact missionary success and derail missionaries in their careers. Second, it will enable leaders to understand best missionary practices that will contribute to a successful completion of a missionary's ministry and longevity of service. Third, it will give missionary leaders tools to use as they visit fields and encounter missionaries who are involved in issues that impact their ability to finish well.

Although this project is targeted to the Asia Pacific Region, the information discovered, tools developed, and processes created will contribute to a greater understanding of the subject of missionary attrition and longevity and will contribute to other AGWM regions' understanding of the issues.

Summary

This chapter dealt with the research process designed to gather the information necessary to complete the project. It examined the problem addressed by the project, as well as the purpose, design, and scope of the project. It dealt with the project's contexts and the major phases that include research, planning, action, and evaluation. The next chapter includes an examination of what occurred during the research, and will include the analysis of the data.

6 RESULTS OF RESEARCHING PERSONNEL RECORDS

This project utilized two types of research. First, analysis of attrition information gleaned from the Assemblies of God World Missions personnel records, which is analyzed here, revealed information about the types of attrition at work in the missionary personnel. The second phase involved the development of a survey instrument that was sent to veteran and retired missionaries who served more than one term of cross-cultural ministry. This will be the subject of the next chapter.

Research of Personnel Records

The AGWM director of personnel and family life gave me access to the personnel records of missionaries who were removed from active missionary status during the twenty-year period under study. These records were reviewed and the reasons for missionary departures were evaluated in order to see if there were any identifiable trends. These trends were classified into five categories: retired, resigned, died, dismissed, and transferred. The information which follows contains the results of this research.

Assemblies of God Missionary Attrition

The AGWM was first organized in 1916, just two years after the beginning of the denomination in 1914. World missions has been a priority since the beginning with missionaries being sent all over the world. AGWM has divided the world into six regions with Asia Pacific identified as one of the regions. There are thirty-five countries within the Asia Pacific Region, which is subdivided into four areas: Northern Pacific Rim, Pacific Oceania, Peninsular Asia, and Southeast Asia.

The Asia Pacific Indigenous Mission Context

Before looking at the statistics within the U.S. Assemblies of God, it is valuable to highlight the growth of indigenous missions worldwide that impacts missions in general. National churches worldwide are sending their own missionaries and are becoming significant partners in missions. The career and associate personnel sent from national churches exceeds the number of missionaries sent from the American Assemblies of God World Missions department, effectively doubling the number of Assemblies of God missionaries serving in cross-cultural missions.

In the Asia Pacific Region, a mission training program (MTP) began in 1995 on the campus of the Asia Pacific Theological Seminary (APTS). During the past 14 years, more than 300 Asian and Pacific Island missionaries received training and were sent out from their home country to other countries as cross-cultural missionaries. In addition, the Assemblies of God in Korea, Philippines, Japan, Malaysia, Indonesia, and others have sent out thousands of cross-cultural missionaries to people groups within Asia and to other areas of the world.

In August 2006, the Fiji Assemblies of God commissioned six couples for service as cross-cultural missionaries in other countries in the Pacific. There are approximately 50 missionaries sent out from AG churches in the Pacific to other island nations. It has been most gratifying to see the growth of missions from countries that formerly viewed themselves as mission fields but now are beginning to recognize the impact they can make as sending nations. Together, they provide a substantial part of the great number of mission personnel serving in Asia and the Pacific. These indigenous missionaries also face issues that affect their longevity, as do AGWM missionaries.

United States Assemblies of God World Missions

Within the American Assemblies of God, there were four regions with 1,394 missionaries worldwide at the beginning of 1986. At the conclusion of 2005, there were six regions with a total of 2,045 missionaries around the world. During that twenty-year period, there was an increase of 651missionaries. Another source of personnel within the Assemblies of God World Missions exists, which is called the Missionary Associates (M.A.) program. It encourages non-credentialed personnel to serve in cross-cultural missions for two or more years. During the twenty-year scope of this project, the M.A. program grew from less than 100 to 615, providing a combined worldwide total of mission personnel of 2,660.

In 1986, the Asia Pacific region had a total of 315 missionaries. The region divided in 2000, with China becoming a separate region called the Northern Asia Region. All of the mission personnel within China and Hong Kong became a part of that new region, and in subsequent years, several others transferred from Asia Pacific to Northern Asia. This study accounts for this change and reports the changed status of the missionaries affected separately.

The two regions maintain fraternal relationship through a variety of associations mandated by their geographic and cultural proximity, such as sharing advanced degree programs, media ministries, and other significant interaction. To provide a full picture of the growth which has occurred in the entire geographic area at the beginning of 1986 and now forming two regions, the total number of mission personnel has grown to 381 career missionaries with an additional 140 missionary associates or a total of 521 personnel on the field in 2006. This number does not include the growing number of national missionary personnel sent out by the Asian and Pacific Oceania national churches to serve within these countries.

My specific research looks at the attrition of American Assemblies of God missionaries within the Asia Pacific Region between the years 1986 and 2006.

Analysis of Missionary Attrition from Personnel Records

From 1986 to 2005, a total of 209 missionaries left missionary service with the Asia Pacific Region. This number does not include the thirty who transferred when China was incorporated into the newly created Northern Asia Region in 2000. At that time, the missionaries that transferred to Northern Asia represented twelve point sixty-one percent of Asia Pacific's missionary personnel. Those missionaries will not be included in this study because the reason for their departure was not related to normal attrition factors, but because of a structural alignment within the Assemblies of God World Missions.

The largest cause of attrition was resignations, with seventy-five missionaries, leaving for that reason. The reasons for resignations varied from taking a pastorate in the United States, marrying a non-missionary while on the field, family matters, and conflict on the field. The second highest recorded reason for leaving was retirement, affecting sixty-four missionary units After that, twenty-seven Asia Pacific missionaries transferred to other AGWM regions (12.92 percent). Many of these missionaries left when China was separated into its own region and missionaries already serving in China were counted as transfers. An additional eighteen missionaries left Asia Pacific because their special assignments were completed, seventeen missionaries died, and six missionaries were dismissed with cause.

To provide a clearer perspective of Asia Pacific missionary departures, missionary attrition has been divided into four five-year segments. From 1986 to 2005, a total of 209 people left the Asia Pacific Region for a variety of reasons.

Table 6.1. 1986 to 2005 missionary personnel loss

1986 to 1990	A loss of 50 missionary personnel
1991 to 1995	A loss of 57 missionary personnel
1996 to 2000	A loss of 50 missionary personnel
2001to 2005	A loss of 52 missionary personnel
1986 to 2005	209 Total Missionary Departures

Chart 6.1. Missionary loss per five-year increment

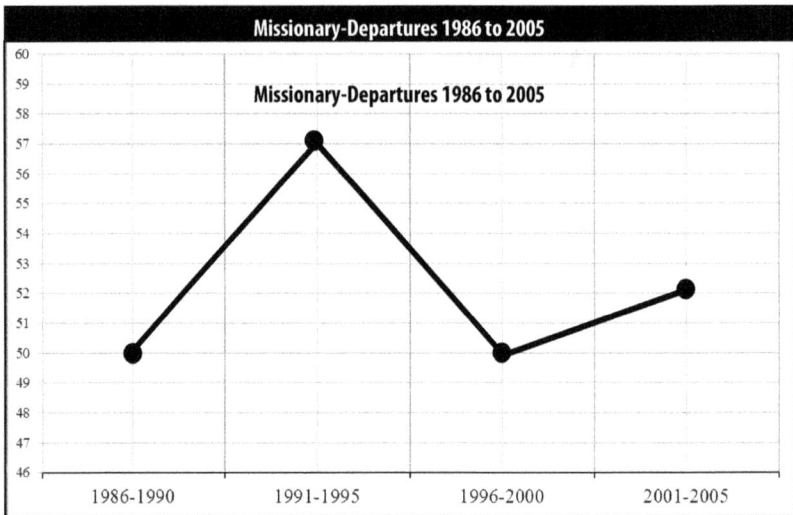

When the departure statistics are broken down into five-year segments (Tables 6.2 through 6.6), the figures look fairly consistent. Dismissals linger at three or below; deaths are fairly consistent except for the 1991 to 1995 cycle, and assignment completions reflects the usage need for targeted needs in the region. However, transfers, retirements, and resignation show some changes from the beginning to the end of the twenty-year cycle.

Table 6.2. 1986 to 1990 missionary attrition grouped by categories

Year	Dismissed	Deceased	Assignment Complete	Transferred	Retired	Resigned
1986	0	1	0	0	5	3
1987	0	2	1	0	1	4
1988	0	0	5	0	4	2
1989	0	0	2	0	2	3
1990	2	0	0	0	5	6
Total:	2	3	8	0	17	18

Table 6.3. 1991 to 1995 missionary attrition grouped by categories

Year	Dismissed	Deceased	Assignment Complete	Transferred	Retired	Resigned
1991	0	2	0	0	2	8
1992	1	3	0	1	6	3
1993	0	0	0	0	2	6
1994	2	3	2	0	6	3
1995	0	0	0	0	3	3
Total:	3	8	2	1	19	23

Table 6.4. 1996 to 2000 missionary attrition grouped by categories

Year	Dismissed	Deceased	Assignment Complete	Transferred	Retired	Resigned
1996	0	2	0	3	4	4
1997	0	1	0	2	3	3
1998	0	0	0	4	2	1
1999	0	0	0	0	0	0
2000	1	0	0	4	7	8
Total:	1	3	0	13	16	16

Table 6.5. 2001 to 2005 missionary attrition grouped by categories

Year	Dismissed	Deceased	Assignment Complete	Transferred	Retired	Resigned
2001	0	1	3	2	3	6
2002	0	0	1	6	2	0
2003	0	0	2	2	1	3
2004	0	1	0	1	2	4
2005	0	1	2	2	1	5
Total:	0	3	8	13	9	18

In the first ten years of the study, there was only one transfer to other regions, while in the second half of the study there were twenty-six. This reflects residual transfers to the newly formed Northern Asia Region as well as attitudinal shifts about missionary service on the field by missionaries and leadership alike. Retirements were consistent for the first fifteen years of the study, dropping to nine in the last five-year cycle, reflecting a demographic shift in the median age of Asia Pacific missionaries. Resignations have remained consistently high throughout the twenty years of the study. In the next section, resignations are examined to identify the reasons so they can be addressed in the region's training program.

Missionary Resignations

During the timeframe of this research, of the 209 missionary units that left Asia Pacific Region, seventy-five were in the form of resignations from AGWM. An examination of the five-year grouping of missionary departures (Tables 6.2 through 6.5) shows eighteen missionaries resigning from 1986 to 1990; twenty-three from 1991 to 1995; sixteen from 1996 to 2000, and eighteen from 2001 to 2006.

Of the missionary units who resigned, some gave more than one reason for leaving. However, there was one main reason that tended to be predominant in their departure. The main reasons for leaving are in the next table, and are grouped into six categories: finances, health, personal reasons, family, transferring to ministries in the United States, and different types of relationship problems.

Table 6.6. Main reasons given for missionary resignations

Years	Finances	Health	Personal	Family	U.S. Ministry	Relationships
1986 - 1990	1	2	5	2	5	5
1991 - 1995	1	1	4	3	4	10
1996 - 2000	0	2	0	2	6	5
2001 - 2005	0	3	0	7	3	4
Total:	2	8	9	14	18	24
Percentage:	2.67%	10.67%	12.00%	18.67%	24.00%	32.00%

Nearly one-third of the units leaving, (32 percent), left because of relationship issues. The types of relationship issues listed in the personnel records were: not getting along with other missionaries or Asia Pacific leadership and conflicts with the national church. Some just did not fit in because of poor communication skills, while some were crippled in building relationships because there were not able to adjust to cross-cultural living and ministry.

In the second ranked reason given for missionary resignations twenty-four percent indicated they were moving back to America to take ministry positions in churches. Any underlying or connected reasons for this were not mentioned in the personnel records. The third most common reason for resigning involved fifteen missionaries (18.67 percent) who left for family reasons such as children's adjustment, schooling, or family problems such as marital issues.

Single Missionary Attrition

In this section, an examination of single missionary departures will identify factors involved in their leaving missionary service in the Asia Pacific region. As of August 2010, there were thirty-two singles serving as appointed personnel in the Asia Pacific Region (see Chart 6.2).

Chart 6.2. Single missionaries by country in 2010.

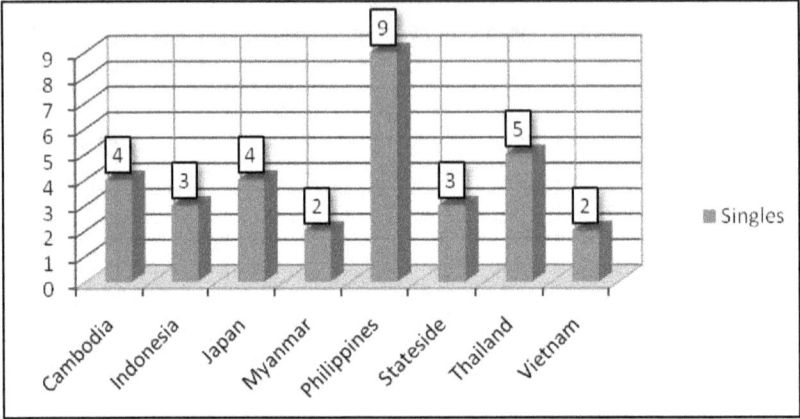

It should be noted that single missionaries are considered the same as married missionaries in terms of being colleagues with the same rights and respect due. Single missionaries serve with the same level of commitment to missions as couples and are as consistent in their length of service. Attrition occurs in single missionaries as well as married couples, although the reasons may differ slightly.

From 1986 to 2005 there were sixty-four single missionaries approved for service in the Asia Pacific region. Of that number, twenty-six were still active as single missionary units in 2009. Missionary records reveal several reasons the missionaries left missions, which includes being uncomfortable serving as single missionaries, conflict with fellow missionaries, completion of assignment, unspecified personal reasons, or relationship problems. Other factors discovered in the personal records were concerns for parents' health, a desire for further education, and plans for marriage. The analysis of single records in five-year increments were categorized as (1) those who were approved, (2) still serving as single missionaries, (3) married, but still serving in missions, (4) married-resigned, or those who left missions for marriage reasons, (5) unknown reasons, and (6) resigned with reasons other than marriage (see Charts 6.3, 6.4, 6.5, and 6.6).

From 1986 to 1990 (see Chart 6.3) there were eleven single missionaries approved for Asia Pacific: seven women and four men. By 2009 there were still three women in missions as singles; three men married while still in missions and later resigned; two women and one man resigned missions to get married; and two women left missions and remained single.

Chart 6.3. 1986 to 1990 single missionary marital status change

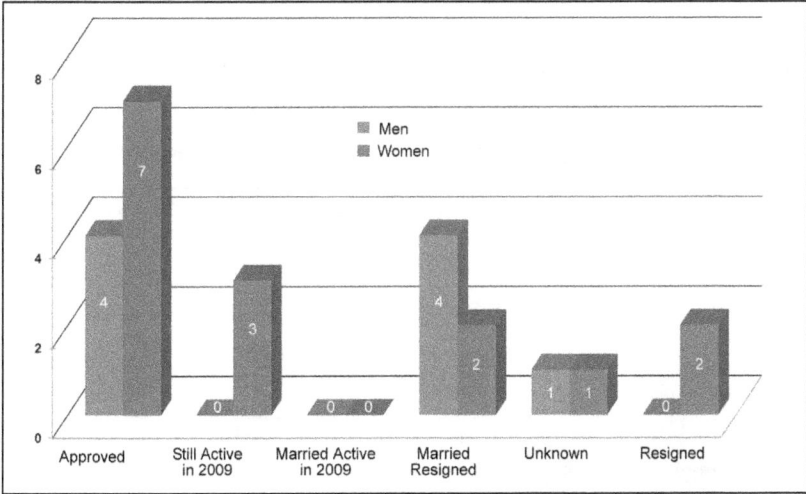

Between 1991 and 1995 (see Chart 6.4) there were twenty-six singles approved for Asia Pacific: fifteen women and eleven men. Five women and two men remained single and in missions; no one married and continued in missions; three men married and left missions; and seven men and 2 women left missions while single.

Chart 6.4. 1991 to 1995 single missionary marital status change

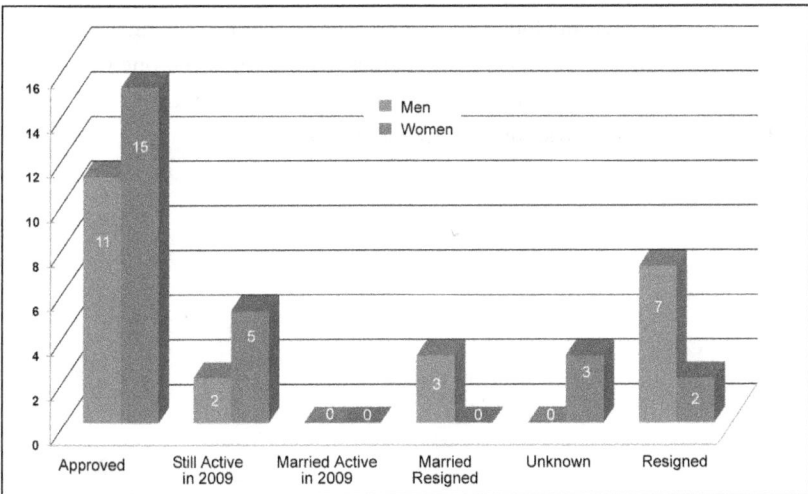

From 1996 to 2000 (see Chart 6.5) a total of seventeen single missionaries were approved for service in the region under study: twelve women and five men. Six women and two men remain single and in missions; three women and two men married and remain in missions; and two left mission service to get married. There was no information on one, while two resigned from missions.

Chart 6.5. 1996 to 2000 single missionary marital status change

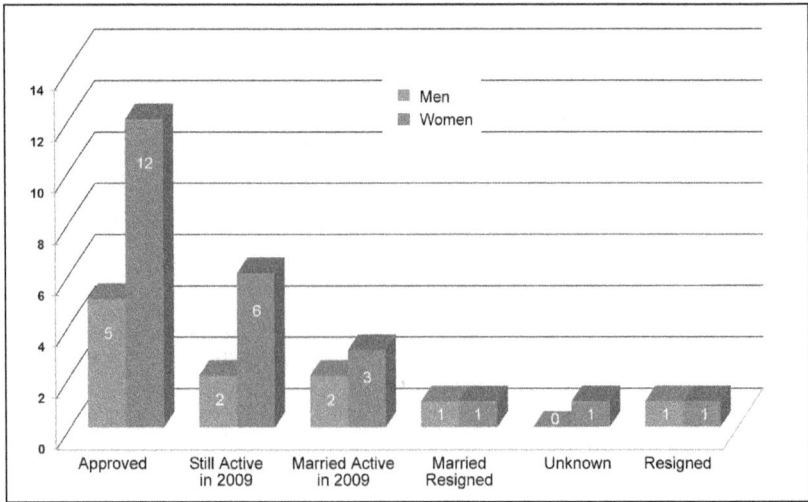

Between 2001 and 2005 (see Chart 6.6) there were ten singles approved for Asia Pacific: six women and four men. Five women and three men remain single and continue in missions. Two resigned to get married: one man and one woman. For two women, it is unknown why they left. There were no resignations that did not involve marriage, with two leaving service for unknown reasons.

Chart 6.6. 2001 to 2005 single missionary marital status change

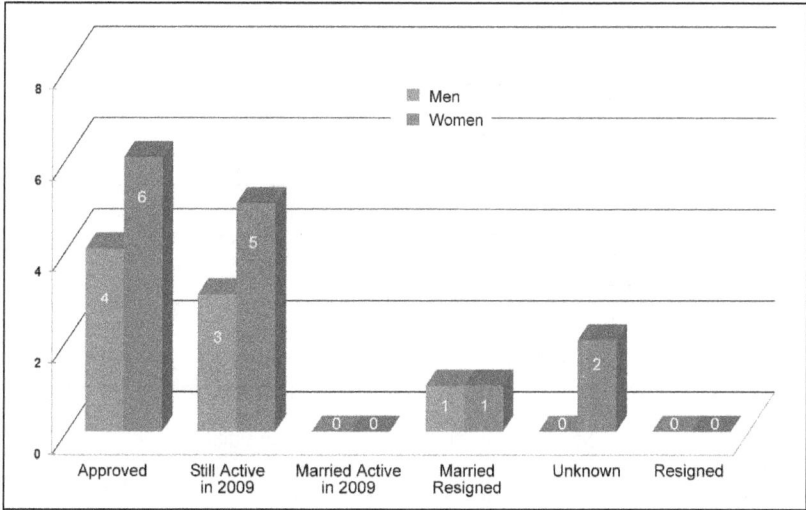

Several interesting statistics were revealed in researching the number of single candidates approved from 1986 to 2005. The largest number of singles approved were in the first five years of the decade of the 1990s (1991 to 1995). That number dropped in each succeeding five year span. From 1986 to 2005, forty single women and twenty-four single men were approved for service in the Asia Pacific Region. Twenty-six (19 women and 7 men) remained single and were still active in missions in 2009. Five married and stayed in missions. Eight left for unknown reasons. Twelve left to get married. The reasons for the remaining thirteen who resigned varied and are cataloged on the following page (see Table 6.8).

Comparison of Married and Single Missionary Resignations

There were sixty-two married missionaries and thirteen singles that resigned for reasons other than marriage in the period under study. The missionaries often gave more than one reason for leaving missionary service. Tables 6.7 and 6.8 detail all the reasons given for resignations.

Table 6.7. Married missionary reasons for resigning

Years	Finances	Health	Personal	Family	U.S. Ministry	Relationships
1986 - 1990	1	1	4	1	4	4
1991 - 1995	1	1	4	2	4	7
1996 - 2000	0	2	0	1	6	5
2001 - 2005	0	2	0	7	3	2
Total:	2	6	8	11	17	18
Percentage:	3.23%	9.68%	12.90%	17.74%	27.42%	29.03%

Table 6.8. Single missionary reasons for resigning

Years	Finances	Health	Personal	Family	U.S. Ministry	Relationships
1986 - 1990	0	1	1	1	1	1
1991 - 1995	0	0	0	1	0	3
1996 - 2000	0	0	0	0	0	0
2001 - 2005	0	1	0	1	0	2
Total:	0	2	1	3	1	6
Percentage:	0%	15.38%	7.69%	23.08%	7.69%	46.15%

The reasons given by married missionaries for resigning were finances, health, personal reasons, family, accepting ministry positions in the United States, and relationship problems. The reasons given by single missionaries were similar although the percentages differed.

When comparing the different reasons married and single missionaries resigned in the tables above as well in Chart 6.7 below a significant difference appears in the area of leaving to minister in the United States. When resigning, twenty-seven point forty-two percent of married missionaries list US ministry as the reason, while only seven point sixty-nine percent of singles list US ministry as the reason. A larger contrast is in relationships. Married missionaries give relationships as the reason (29.03 percent) less than single missionaries (46.15 percent).

Chart 6.7. Comparison of Married and Single Missionaries resignation reasons

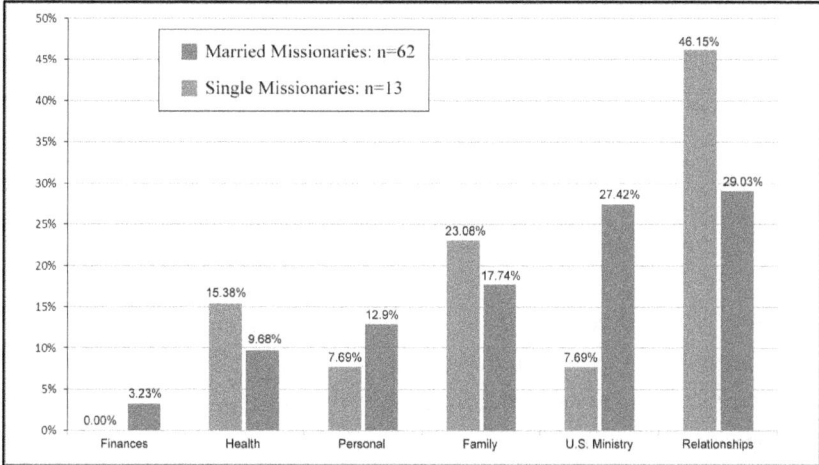

This is significant because relationships are important to both married and single missionaries, but seems to be significantly more important to singles. When it comes to creating conditions leading to resignations, it seems to have the greatest impact upon singles. This indicates a need to help new missionaries understand the importance for developing relationships while in the field during Asia Pacific regional training programs for new candidates for the field. Relationships, along with the related subject of conflict and conflict management are addressed in the training sessions for new missionaries and the on-going training for veteran missionaries in the Asia Pacific region.

Summary

Phase one of the field research into Asia Pacific missionary attrition reveals a consistent loss of missionaries over the years (Table 6.1). The study of personnel records involving 209 missionary units and covering a twenty- year time span reveals several reasons for the loss with retirement and resignations as the largest causes. Other reasons were statistically small with dismissals being two point eighty-seven percent and death eight point thirteen percent of the reasons. There does not seem much can be done about the deaths other than providing the medical insurance already provided to the missionary family. However, the causes of dismissals warrant investigation because of the moral or relational implications and the effect they have on the national church's view of the missionary force and on the morale of those remaining on the field. These are causes that can and should be addressed through the missional training processes offered by the Asia Pacific region for new and veteran missionaries. The third most common reason for loss of missionaries to the Asia Pacific region was transferring to other regions. The reasons for this also warrant further investigation to see what role conflict with others or job satisfaction plays in missionaries leaving the region. These are issues that can be addressed during new missionary training and in on-going training sessions at Missionary Renewal or during field meetings. The second highest reason for leaving was retirement (29.19 percent). This is the direct result of longevity of service. The survey instrument developed and used in the second stage of this research provided helpful information about how these people successfully maintained a career in missionary service.

The highest scoring reason for missionary attrition was resignation, comprising thirty-six point eighty-four percent of those leaving in the personnel records. The reasons missionaries resigned listed in the personnel records fit into six categories: finances (2.60) percent; health (10.39 percent); personal reasons (11.69 percent); family related issues (19.48 percent); transfer to U. S. ministry (23.38 percent); and relationship problems (32.47 percent). The knowledge gained from the records about the resignations is addressed in the training and sessions developed for new and veteran missionaries.

When contrasting the reasons missionaries resigned between married and single missionaries, it was found that family and relationship issues were significantly higher for singles. Transferring to U. S. ministry was a major factor for married missionaries—over one-quarter of them (27.42 percent)—compared to one single missionary giving this as a reason for resignation in the twenty- year span of this research. The results of this study show there are differing reasons between single and married missionaries for resigning.

There are three main areas identified from the analysis of missionary personnel in the time period under study that should be addressed in training new missionaries when they arrive on the field and used with on-going preparation of veterans.

- Health. This includes preventable health issues that relate to the long-term physical and emotional health of the missionary and his family.

- Family related issues. This includes the families' well-being, children's schooling, and aging parents in America.
- Relationships. This includes relationships between other AG missionaries, non-AG missionaries, AGWM leadership, Asia Pacific regional leadership, and the national church.

The next chapter will look at phase two of the field research, which deals with veteran missionary longevity factors, based on the results of surveys that were sent to these missionaries, both active and retired.

7 RESULTS FROM VETERAN MISSIONARIES SURVEY QUESTIONS

Surveys were sent to missionaries asking them questions about what caused them to serve and to stay on the field. Two types of missionaries were surveyed: veterans who were still active but with more than one complete term of service; and missionaries who retired from active missionary service. There were seven questions that asked them to write answers about longevity and three quantitative questions utilizing Likert scales. Below are the results that have been compiled.

Question one asked their years of service. The thirty-two respondents had an average of nearly twenty years of tenure, with the high being thirty-three years and the lowest eight. Question two asked them to describe their current job description. The respondents listed children's ministry, teaching, church planting, country moderator, health care ministry, Bible school administration, deaf ministry, crusade preaching, and discipleship as primary duties.

Results from Qualitative Longevity Questions

Questions three, four, five, nine, and ten are qualitative questions that ask for a written response from the missionary. These questions are analyzed in this section.

Question Three: "List the top five factors that have helped you to remain in missions."

Table 7.1: Responses to Question Three

Number	Question Three Answers	Percentage
37	Call of God	94.87 %
34	Relationships	87.18 %
22	Spirituality	56.41 %
19	Sense of Self Worth	48.72 %
14	AGWM Support	35.90 %
12	Finances	30.77 %
5	Family	12.82%

The respondents here listed the call of God as most important to longevity. The respondents rated relationships as the next important factor in their longevity at eighty-seven point eighteen percent. Their responses in this area include relationships with other AGWM missionaries, non-AGWM missionaries, expatriates, and nationals. They indicate that field and area meetings are important for relationship building. This was followed by spirituality as the third most important element in their longevity. The relationship between a sense of the call of God and spirituality and piety indicates the need for emphasis on spiritual renewal and commitment in the training sessions for new missionaries and an on-going reminder in the region's regular meetings involving veteran missionaries. This is in line with what other researchers found regarding the importance of God's call to missionaries' sense of purpose.[1] This sense of purpose enables missionaries to stand and serve in spite of challenges.

Additional responses included a sense of self-worth as important to longevity. They wrote that a sense of accomplishment, seeing fruit from their ministry, and feeling that they are filling a real need helped them feel valued as missionaries and individuals. This indicates a need for AGWM leadership to know of the need to communicate self-worth to their missionary team and to monitor the attitudes of personnel so that help is given in this area. This also indicates that training be given in these areas during new missionary training sessions and also included in regular missionary meetings involving veterans.

---

[1] Hesselgrave, *Communicating Christ Cross-Culturally*, 405; Rance, *The Empowered Call*, 34–36.

Others wrote that feeling supported by AGWM leadership and programs were important to their longevity. This included a feeling of being a part of a team, being involved in meeting felt needs of the area or country in which they lived, and the help they receive from AGWM in times of ministry or personal crisis. Finances were also an important factor in missionary longevity, with thirty point seventy-seven percent indicating that a solid support base emanating from home churches and districts was crucial to their tenure. This indicates that new missionaries and veterans alike should be given training on best practices in raising funds from their support base using current technologies or methodologies.

Respondents to the survey expressed their feelings about the importance of relationships. One said, "I am much more aware that it is relationships first, last, and always that really make a difference in ministry longevity and effectiveness." Another stated, "We have learned to place more importance on people and relationship over structure and things." Another expressed appreciation for AGWM leadership: "The AG missionary leadership, during my twenty-six years of ministry, has held to a priority of values: God-family-ministry. Because of this, I have been able to 'have a sense of family life' while fulfilling my lifetime commitment to the call of missions." One told of growth culturally: "Having grown up in a small, close-knit community, living on the mission field has ... broadened my horizons and taught me to have a tolerance and open mind towards people ... different from me. I now have a greater appreciation for different cultures and have learned to better adapt to ... working with people from many different countries and backgrounds."

Question Four: "What do you consider the greatest challenge that could have taken you out of missions during each term?"

Table 7:2 Responses to Question Four

Number	Question Four Responses	Percentage
25	Family	64.10 %
16	Work Conditions	41.03 %
11	Relationships	28.21 %
9	AGWM Support	23.08 %
8	Finances	20.51 %
8	Spirituality	20.51 %

The responses to question four indicate that the most critical issue they had to overcome was family related challenges (64.2 percent). These ranged from children's needs—schooling, behavior problems, special needs child, and lengthy separation from children—to health issues, aging parents, and marriage problems. Work conditions were the second highest area of stress (41.03 percent). The respondents mentioned over-work, burnout, living conditions, cultural adjustment, language study, and national political issues as points of stress affecting their peace of mind. Relationships, or more specifically, broken relationships due to conflict, were the next area of stress followed by AGWM support, finances, and spiritual issues.

The respondents to this study are consistent with the results of studies conducted by Storti and Rosik and Pandzic,[2] which indicate the need for an active support mechanism to enhance the missionaries' experience on the field and to provide counseling in areas involving their families and children, workloads, health issues, and finances. There is a need for counseling services provided and ready sources of information for missionaries in need of help. Foyle indicates that these stressors can be turned into positive attitudes with proper responses.[3]

Survey respondents shared some of their difficult times. One family shared:

> There were a few times when we faced challenging times with our children, school situations, and no foreign friends because of the small number of missionaries. Our kids had challenges with the culture and living conditions in the early years. For us, most of these were answered in time and through prayer. There were times that the load of the work was so much, along with all the legal obligations for our visa, that we wondered if we could . . . maintain a healthy family. God has done so much for our family in meeting each challenge but I know that any of the issues could have kept us from moving on to another term.

Another family stated: "Our children's schooling and needs was an important issue. I realize that even though my wife and me are called, the kids are along for the ride . . . Educating your children properly, health situations, and distance from their family in the USA are all sacrifices that are hard to make."

Another family had a positive experience with children's schooling:

> We are thankful that AGWM allows us to choose the best type of schooling for our kids. In our case, our son went to a boarding school in

[2] Storti, 2–10; Rosik and Pandzic, 3–5.
[3] Foyle, 14

Malaysia, our middle child homeschooled through 10ᵗʰ grade and then transferred to international school. We were allowed to stay on a 5ᵗʰ year so she could graduate from that school. Our youngest homeschooled through 3ʳᵈ grade and then attended international school. They all came through with flying colors.

One family said, "We have a special needs son, and had we not found a good situation for him, we would have moved back to the US for his wellbeing." Concerning finances, another family shared:

> We have come close a couple of times of not having needed funds for our budget. It adds a huge stress constantly working to have enough funds, especially when you are supervising large projects. We had a strong team back home praying for us and we knew we could go to them at any time there were special needs, and we did this. If we had not had this, it would have been easy to fall out.

Some survey respondents shared personal crises. One person said, "I had a personal crisis in my life . . . I could have been lost to ministry . . . the personnel and family program . . . facilitated my acquiring the counseling I needed to heal and move forward." Another person stated, "I am a single missionary. Several years ago, I found my mother entering the last stages of cancer . . . Had my mission board not given me time to be with her . . . and then allowed me time with my father when she died six months later, I would have been hard pressed to continue in missions."

Question Five: "What do you (family) do to relieve stress, find relaxation, and renew focus?"

Table 7.3. Responses to Question Five

Number	Question Five Answers	Percentage
27	Home/Family Activities	69.2 %
19	Social Activities	48.7 %
18	Physical Games and Exercise	46.2 %
17	Short Family Trips	43.6 %
10	Religious Activities	25.6 %
7	Vacations	17.9 %
1	MRAP	2.6 %

The responses to question five indicate that the mechanisms to relieve stress on the field involve family activities including watching television or videos, playing games, hobbies, talking with the kids, spouse, or grandchildren, reading, or cooking. Social activities were second in importance. These include eating out and fellowshipping with other missionaries and nationals. This is followed by physical games and exercise such as golf, tennis, basketball, walking on the beach, or bike riding and then short family trips including avocational activities such devotion and prayer, ministering, and attending retreats, and family vacations. One mentioned attending counseling at the Missionary Renewal Asia Pacific Center (MRAP), and AGWM ministry in Kirkland, Washington.

All of this information indicates that new missionaries should learn the value of stress reduction. There should be a venue for veteran missionaries to talk to younger missionaries about how to reduce stress. Counseling involving stress management principles that include the above-mentioned means should also be a part of new missionary training. Also, when AGWM leaders encounter missionaries on the field who do not manage stress adequately, they should be in a position to counsel ways to reduce stress.

Question Nine: "How has the Holy Spirit provided guidance, insight, and anointing to do your work in missions?"

Table 7.4: Responses to Question Nine

Number	Question Five Answers	Percentage
32	Guidance	82.1 %
17	Enablement	43.6 %
14	Comfort and protection	35.9 %
11	Miracles	28.2 %
2	Nothing	5.1 %

The responses indicate an overwhelming reliance upon the Holy Spirit for personal and ministry guidance. This is followed by dependence upon the Holy Spirit for divine enablement through anointing in ministry, open doors, and discernment, and the operation of the gifts of the Spirit. Comfort and protections was another important link with the Holy Spirit for protection, encouragement, emotional healing, and comfort. Miracles were also indicated as how the Spirit helps in difficult situations in cross-cultural life and ministry. Two Pentecostal missionaries, interestingly enough, said they could not think of anything or left it blank.

The dynamic of the Holy Spirit in missionary longevity is only cursorily addressed in literature about missionary attrition and longevity. While some address the spirituality of missionaries as a factor[4] and Rance, a Pentecostal missiologist, accentuates the importance of the Holy Spirit in the call of God to missions and the missionary's reliance upon the Spirit during their service for empowerment and strength,[5] little is said about reliance upon the Holy Spirit by other Evangelical authors or the importance of the Holy Spirit to missionary longevity. Because this is a study about a Pentecostal mission sending body, staffed by Pentecostal missionaries, it is interesting to note that in spite of its absence in the authoritative books on the subject, veteran Pentecostal missionaries believe the Holy Spirit's work in their lives is a significant factor in their longevity.

It was interesting to read the survey responses to God's miraculous intervention in the lives of Asia Pacific missionaries. One person shared, "The main ministry of the Holy Spirit to us has been to give us wisdom in making decisions that affected not only the future of our work, but the future of the field. There have been occasions when we were able to supernaturally discern things in people's lives which have enabled us to minister to them effectively." Another person said:

> ... there is no distance in prayer and God always knows our needs. This became real to us on one occasion when we were being shot at while conducting a service at a village church here in our country. The house was damaged but we were all spared as we found out later ... a small AG church in Tennessee had been led of the Lord to pray for our protection by a message in tongues and interpretation during one of their services.

Another person in a desperate circumstance shared:

> While living in a bush village I saw the protection of the Holy Spirit to preserve my life when an islander was only about 8 feet from where I stood, swinging a machete [and] yelling 'I'm going to kill that missionary.' However, he could not see me though [sic] I was very close and he was later taken to jail. Later we found out while in jail he gave his life to Christ.

---

[4] Stoddard, *The Heart of Mentoring*, 11–12, 211; Taylor, "Introduction: Examining the Iceberg Called Attrition," 12; Taylor, "Challenging the Missions Stakeholders, 358.
[5] Rance, 34–36

Another missionary stated: "Being single, there have been many times the Lord has closed my ears and closed my eyes to what was happening around me. After seeing the news later, I realized the Lord was protecting me every step of the way. The Holy Spirit speaks to me as I am driving, directing to stay clear of certain danger areas..."

Question Ten: "In what ways has your years in missions changed your perspective in life?"

Table 7.5: Responses to Question Ten

Number	Question Ten Answers	Percentage
25	More Relational	64.1 %
24	More Culturally Aware	61.5 %
20	More Spiritually Minded	41.0 %
9	More Self-Aware	25.6 %
9	More Ministry and Mission Awareness	25.6 %
1	More Cynical	2.6 %

These responses indicate that missionaries who serve a long time are changed by the experience. The respondents stated they were more relational. This included relationships within their family, other missionary team members, and a greater compassion for the needs of other. They indicated they were more culturally aware of their own Western culture and appreciative of other cultures, as well as feeling that their cultural horizons have been broadened. The next highest responses indicated they were more spiritually aware, with a greater awareness of the spiritual warfare existing in the world, and having a greater appreciation of the body of Christ and the value of harmony in the church. Self-awareness is another area that years of missionary service changed the respondent's life. Along with this, there is a heightened understanding of ministry and missions. On the other hand, one respondent reported they were more cynical now after their years of missionary service.

These responses indicate a change within the missionary as his or her time of service lengthens. This includes relationship with God, other cultures, and other people. This seems to indicate that personal growth in the matter of personal piety, cultural appreciation, and relationships are important to missionary longevity. Asia Pacific leadership can help new missionaries address this through teaching, counseling, and interaction with veteran missionaries.

Results from Quantitative Longevity Questions

Questions six to eight required responses questions weighted on a scale from one being the lowest and five the highest rating. The responses are discussed in the following sections.

Question Six: "Would you rate the following from one (low) to five (high) in positive encouragement?"

Chart 7.1: Responses to question six

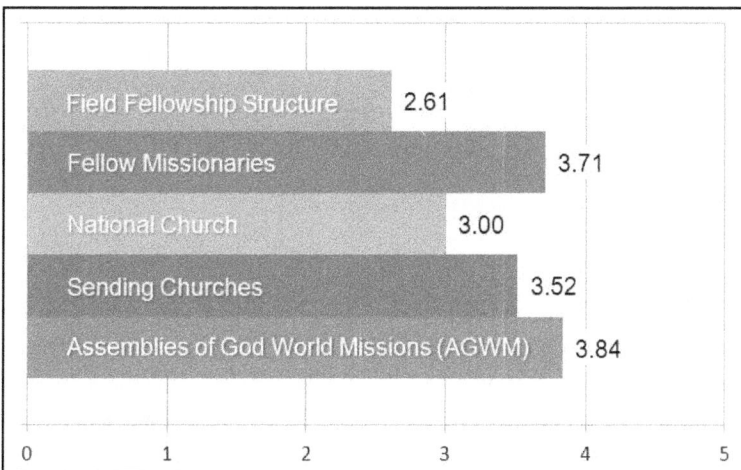

Field Fellowship Structure	2.61
Fellow Missionaries	3.71
National Church	3.00
Sending Churches	3.52
Assemblies of God World Missions (AGWM)	3.84

AGWM received the highest ranking, which speaks well of the efforts made by Asia Pacific's leadership team consisting of the regional director, area directors, and Asia Pacific office staff; although there is still room for improvement. Field fellowship structures scored the lowest, indicating the need for training for field leadership in how to respond to missionary issues and questions.

Question Seven: "How would you rate AGWM as an organization in the below listed areas?" A score of one is low and five is high.

Chart 7.2: Responses to question seven

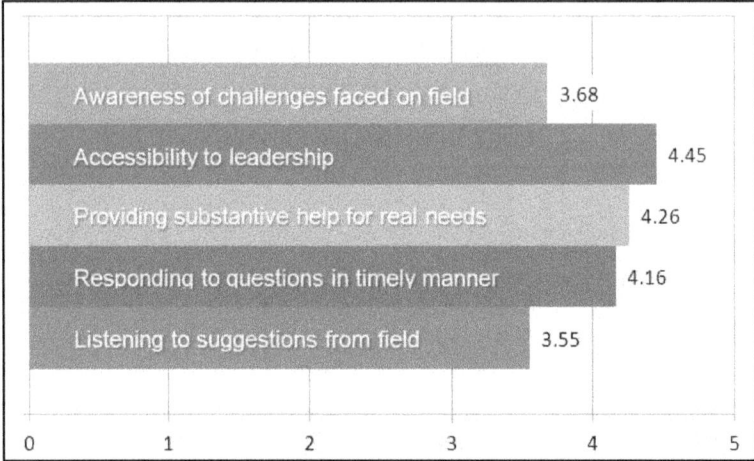

Category	Score
Awareness of challenges faced on field	3.68
Accessibility to leadership	4.45
Providing substantive help for real needs	4.26
Responding to questions in timely manner	4.16
Listening to suggestions from field	3.55

Accessibility to leadership scored the highest, which speaks well of the openness stressed by regional leadership, which is the missionaries' direct link to AGWM. While listening to suggestions on the field was the lowest, it was still fairly high, indicating that efforts are being made to be responsive to missionary questions and needs. However, it is low enough to warrant a concerted effort to address this by bringing it to the attention of regional leadership and staff.

Each of the scores on this question are fairly high, which gives the regional leadership team reason for thankfulness for past leadership commitments towards transparency and responsiveness, and optimistic about the future of regional missionary and Asia Pacific leadership team interaction.

Question Eight: "How would you rate the following factors in importance to your longevity in missions?"

Chart 7.3: Responses to question eight

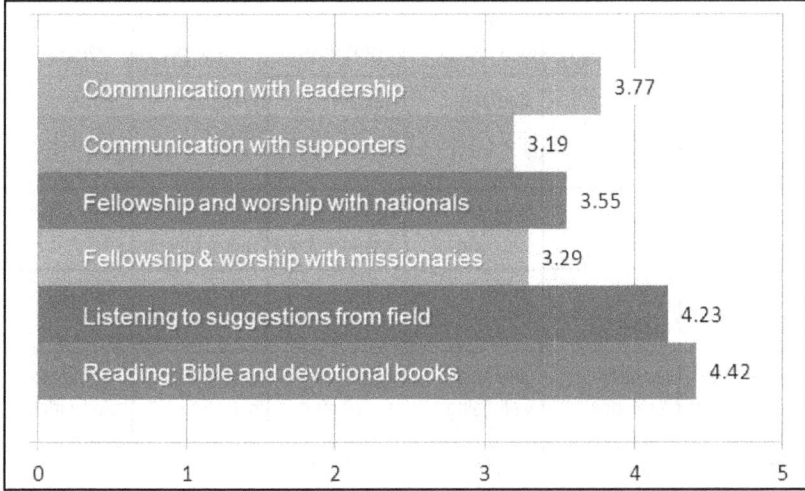

Factor	Score
Communication with leadership	3.77
Communication with supporters	3.19
Fellowship and worship with nationals	3.55
Fellowship & worship with missionaries	3.29
Listening to suggestions from field	4.23
Reading: Bible and devotional books	4.42

The fact that all of these numbers are fairly high is encouraging. However, anything over four is excellent; three to four is good but with room for improvement; and anything below three indicates there is definite room for improvement. Nothing was identified that indicated a serious problem.

Since this question addresses missionary longevity directly and is asked of religious workers, the fact that reading the Bible and devotional books scored high is not a surprise. The fact that communication with supporters scored the lowest, while at the same time being the main way that missionaries maintain their support, indicates the need for further study to discover why this is so. It also indicates the need to address this in the training sessions with new missionaries and during open meetings with the missionary body, which includes new and veteran missionaries. It is interesting that listening to suggestions from the field scored as high as it did. It indicates the importance for regional, area, and field leadership to be open and transparent in their communication with missionaries and open to suggestions.

Summary

Phase two of the field research revealed important reasons why missionaries stayed.

Table 7.6: Important Components that Contribute to Missionary Longevity

Piety	Relationships	Family	Holy Spirit	Finances	Adapting
God's call	Other AG and non-missionaries	Marriage	Guidance	Personal finances	Culture shock
Personal Devotions	National Church	Children's schooling	Miraculous interventions	District and church support	Language
Great Commission	AGWM leadership	Health	Anointing	Deputation	Homesick
Dependence on God	Conflict resolution skills	Emotional well-being	Protection and comfort	Correct use of money	Learning to relax with the family

Among the significant reasons were personal piety and a sense of God's call to missions. Associated with this was a concern for a sense of accomplishment; they wanted to know they were making a difference and doing something beneficial. Relationships were a significant factor in missionary longevity. The relationship with AGWM leadership was important, with the need expressed for two-way communication and a sense that the missionary was being heard by his leaders. Relationships with other missionaries and the national church were also important to missionary longevity. All of these longevity factors are incorporated into the training sessions for new and veteran missionaries developed by this project. Factors important to missionary longevity identified in this study include:

- A missionary's relationship with God. Personal piety includes a focus on God's call to cross-cultural ministry, personal devotion, an understanding of the Great Commission, and a dependence upon God in his or her daily life.
- Relationships with other AG missionaries, the national church, AGWM leadership. Associated with this in the relationship arena is the development of conflict resolution skills for use within the missionary context as well as in the national church.

- Family issues. This includes marriage relationships between couples, children's issues, such as schooling, health factors involving the missionary and his children, and emotional well-being of the family.
- Reliance upon the Holy Spirit. Factors crucial to this are relying on the Holy Spirit for guidance, miraculous interventions, anointing for service, and protection and comfort. The Holy Spirit also helps committed missionaries during their adjustment period to deal with stress during their devotion times, deal with relationship issues, and to have the ability to forgive others for perceived or real slights.
- Financial stability in the missionary's ability to handle personal and work finances. This includes a focus on maintaining his or her district and home churches confidence and support, an understanding of how to make the most of deputation, and how to handle money correctly.
- Adapting to cross-cultural life and ministry. It is important missionaries are able to deal with culture shock, language acquisition, and homesickness. An associated factor identified in this research was the missionary's ability to learn how to relax with his family.

This chapter described the results of phase two of the field research, which focused on the analysis of the survey instrument sent to veteran missionaries. There were several longevity factors that were identified in this phase, which were incorporated into this project's training program developed for new and veteran missionaries. The next chapter will describe a project strategy for missionary longevity, including the rationale for training sessions, how they were structured, outlines of these sessions, and what topics were taught.

8 A STRATEGY FOR LONGEVITY

This chapter describes a project that assists Asia Pacific missionaries in adapting to the stresses involved in cross-cultural ministry in an effort to enable them to successfully complete their missionary calling. The purpose of this study is to evaluate the factors that result in missionary attrition within the Asia Pacific Region with the goal of helping more personnel finish well in their missionary careers.

Overview of the Project Strategy for Missionary Longevity

The project's methodology includes teaching and counseling sessions that address the issues identified in the research chapters and occurring in venues that coincide with times associated with AGWM's annual missionary training sessions for new missionaries who have not yet completed one term of missionary service and the Regional Studies sessions for all missionaries in attendance that occur during Missionary Renewal sessions. These two groups combine the target audience of the strategy for increasing longevity. The training is based on factors discovered in the research aspect of the project associated with helping missionaries serve longer and finish well. The issues that are dealt with were identified in the research described in chapters six and seven. These issues are categorized into six areas of focus.

Table 8.1. Important Components that Contribute to Missionary Longevity

Piety	Relationships	Family	Holy Spirit	Finances	Adapting
God's call	Other AG and non-missionaries	Marriage	Guidance	Personal finances	Culture shock
Personal Devotions	National Church	Children's schooling	Miraculous interventions	District and church support	Language
Great Commission	AGWM leadership	Health	Anointing	Deputation	Homesick
Dependence on God	Conflict resolution skills	Emotional well-being	Protection and comfort	Correct use of money	Learning to relax with the family

The Issues Addressed in the Project

The issues addressed here for increased missionary longevity are those identified in the research and are categorized as piety, relationships, family, Holy Spirit, and adapting. These issues will concentrate on the following areas:

1. Instruction on missionary piety delves into the missionary call, the Great Commission, personal devotions, and dependence on God.

2. Missionary relationships concentrate on relationships between other AG missionaries and non-AG missionaries, the national church, the AGWM leadership and conflict resolution.

3. The missionary family was another factor identified as an important component in missionary longevity. It will concentrate on the missionary's marriage, children's schooling, the health of the missionary family, and the family's emotional well-being.

4. Being Pentecostal, the missionaries indicated that the Holy Spirit was an important part of missionary success and longevity. The action concerning the Holy Spirit focuses on the Spirit's guidance of missionary efforts and decisions, miraculous interventions in the missionary's life and ministry, the Spirit's anointing, and the Spirit's protection and comfort.

5. Missionary finance was indicated as an important factor in missionary success and longevity. The financial aspect of missions deals with personal finances, district and church support, deputation, and the correct use of money.

6. The ability of the missionary to adapt to his new environment and ministry examines culture shock, language acquisition, homesickness, and learning to relax as a family.

Project Strategy, Methodology, and Venues

The six issues that impact missionary longevity are addressed in a strategy that involves teaching by people with expertise in the identified areas, intentional interaction with area directors and veteran missionaries, and interaction with counselors.

Table 8.2. Implementation areas of strategy for missionary longevity

Missionary Training	Regional Studies	On-field Meetings	Counseling
Culture shock	Emotional health (Issues such as expectations)	Interaction with AGWM leadership	Emotional health counseling
Financial skills	Physical health	Relationship building	Crisis counseling
Conflict management	Conflict management	Conflict management	Children's education counseling
Relationship building	Relationship building and interpersonal skills	Learning to take care of themselves (relaxation)	Marriage counseling
Spiritual emphasis	Spiritual emphasis	Spiritual emphasis	Trauma counseling

Four venues are utilized in the research here. The first two venues will involve the Assemblies of God World Missions annual Missionary Training and Regional Studies sessions that are already set aside for missionary preparation and training. The project's impact on these sessions is in focus, purpose, and the direction of the teaching.

1. New missionary training sessions, attended by newly approved missionaries and conducted in Springfield, Missouri will address culture shock, financial skills, conflict management, relationship building, and emphasize spiritual piety.

2. Regional studies sessions will involve new and veteran missionaries in meetings held during the annual Missionary Renewal sessions in Springfield, Missouri. These meetings will focus on the missionary's

emotional and physical health, conflict management, relationship building, and personal piety. The topics for regional studies and on-field meetings also reflect the research data on the primary reasons for attrition and recommendations from veteran missionaries for longevity.

3. On-field meetings are a part of the strategy to implement instruction on the identified issues (see Table 8.1). The meetings are implemented in conjunction with established field retreats, country gatherings, and visitations by the Regional Director. In the on-field setting, the missionary's interaction with AGWM leadership, relationship building between the missionary family and the national church, conflict management, learning how to relax, and personal piety are addressed.

4. Counseling, as a part of the overall strategy for missionary longevity, is implemented in conjunction with my office as Asia Pacific Regional Director, Asia Pacific Area Directors, and Missionary Renewal Asia Pacific (MRAP), which is a counseling and missionary wellness ministry sponsored by the Asia Pacific Region. The strategy will include (a) interventions for missionaries who are involved in life situations that threaten to cut short their missionary careers and (b) teaching sessions conducted in on-field settings that focus on emotional health, and counseling in the areas of missionary crisis, children's education, marriage, and trauma. The topics selected for counseling represent areas where specialized expertise can assist couples, families, and singles in meeting missionary needs and assist in building missionary longevity. These areas include emotional health counseling, crisis counseling, children's education counseling, marriage counseling, and trauma counseling.

Missionary Training and Renewal

The first implementation of the project's strategy occurred June 2010. New missionaries gathered for the required Missionary Training, Missionary Renewal, and Regional Studies sessions. The sessions are divided between AGWM personnel instructing new missionaries on issues related to missionary life in general and the Asia Pacific Region. The regional sessions were utilized to implement the strategy for missionary longevity in the region.

New Missionary Training

New missionary training was the focus of AGWM's Missionary Training sessions in June 2011. Imbedded in these sessions were times dedicated to each region's particular focus. Designing a program of new missionary training that facilitates longevity of service and lessens the likelihood of failure was established with best practices for missionary retention foremost in mind. The regional director, area directors, and veteran missionaries were recruited to assist with teaching assignments and to interact with the new missionaries for times of mentoring.

The formal new missionary training sessions covered a number of areas that impact missionary longevity. These include:

1. The region's missional vision and the Asia Pacific's missionary strategy
2. The historical development of Asia Pacific's mission fields
3. The concept of the Asia Pacific missionary team
4. Unreached people groups and the region's efforts to reach them
5. Church planting and church planting movements
6. Culture shock and cultural dynamics as a cross-cultural worker
7. Stressors involved in cross-cultural living and working
8. Tips for life in a cross-cultural setting from Duane Elmer's book *Cross Cultural Connections*
9. Missionary relationships within the Assemblies of God and with missionaries from other organizations and countries
10. Conflict management
11. Missionary family life—including marriages, families, child rearing and children's educational needs
12. Being single in a foreign culture
13. Relationships with the national church.

The new missionary training sessions were interspersed with periods set aside to answer questions the new missionaries asked. General discussions were encouraged and small group sessions were established in which new missionaries were combined with veterans to discuss pertinent issues evolving from the formal sessions and the general group discussions. An exit survey filled out by the participants assessed the sessions so that the program can be improved for subsequent sessions. This is an on-going process, as the Asia Pacific missionary retention program remains relevant to new missionary needs and thus more effective in achieving the goal of greater retention of Asia Pacific missionaries.

Training for Veteran and New Missionaries

During AGWM's annual Missionary Renewal sessions, time is set aside for each region to meet with their missionaries. These meetings are called Regional Studies and the agenda is established by the regional director. The 2010 and 2011 sessions were dedicated to dealing with issues that impact missionary attrition. The sessions were directed to veteran missionaries, transitioning personnel, new missionaries, and missionary mentors and leaders.

As a part of the program to retain missionaries, Drs. Nathan Davis and Jack Rozell were recruited to teach on missionary retention issues. They taught from the book *Resilience: How to Bounce Back* (Beth and Nathan Davis 2010). Nathan Davis is an Assemblies of God missionary who works for Caring Connection and came into missions following retirement from the military where he assisted military personnel in dealing with trauma and crisis. He was trained to prepare military personnel, mentally and physically, to deal with stress. Jack Rozell is director of Missionary Renewal, Asia Pacific (MRAP), which specializes in missionary emotional health and deals directly with attrition issues through the counseling services offered by MRAP. Rozell is also director of Ministry Resources International, which provides emotional health and relationship resources globally. Both Davis and Rozell are eminently qualified to teach Asia Pacific missionaries on issues that might derail their missionary careers.

Missionary attrition issues were addressed by providing new and veteran missionaries with information to help them develop best practices in their professional and personal lives to handle stress and prevent burnout and early departure. The premise of the seminar is that stress is a part of living cross-culturally, but it is possible to build an inner resilience that will enable the missionary to bounce back from crisis situations.

The teaching entailed five hours of instruction over two days and focused on six lifestyle factors that effectively deal with stress and contribute to cross-cultural living success. The lifestyle factors include choices in how one lives by getting proper exercise every day, taking Omega–3, a vitamin supplement, to improve one's health, getting the proper amount of sleep, being exposed to at least fifteen minutes of direct sunlight every day (outdoor activities are good for the body and ultimately a person's mental health), socializing with people other than your family (national and expatriate friends), and being careful to avoid obsessive negative thinking because it leads to depression. Missionaries were taught to deal with negative issues by putting those issues aside and ruminating on positive things.

Field-Based Training and Renewal

Training sessions conducted at field-based venues makes it possible to deal with real-life missionary situations that may impact missionary longevity. The strategy to enable and strengthen Asia Pacific missionaries to endure the stresses and hardships of cross-cultural ministry is also carried out during on-field training sessions for new missionaries and during missionary retreats that include new and veteran missionaries.

On-Field Training for New Missionaries

Orientation meetings for new missionaries are conducted by Asia Pacific area directors for the purpose of helping new missionaries become acclimated to their new life-setting and cross-cultural ministry. These meetings are intended to provide new missionaries with an understanding of what to expect now that they have arrived on the field. While not each Asia Pacific area will do these orientations in the exact same way, Southeast Asia and Peninsular Asia do target their people for training. The training in these sessions includes the following information.

1. They will start each session with devotions and prayer. This is done to emphasize the spiritual nature of all the work because the results of the research in Chapter 4 indicates: (a) a sense of purpose engendered from a reliance upon the Spirit, (b) the sense of divine calling that comes from communing with Christ; and (c) spiritual involvement by the missionary is crucial to their longevity.

2. A description of the area structure and job descriptions. (a) This will include a reminder of the descriptions of the AGWM macro committees and personnel such as the AGWM executive director, the world missions committee, and the regional office. (b) The job descriptions of the AGWM micro-committees and personnel that impact their particular area. This includes the area office, area committees, and any field offices or committees that may exist in the area and how they all relate to each other. (c) The job descriptions, methods of appointment, and term of office of area and field personnel are also examined. This includes the area director, area staff, country moderators, and any field staff that may exist.

3. The forms and functions of the area approvals are identified and discussed. This includes the criteria, forms needed, terminology used, and methods for applying for approvals. This includes approvals for travel outside the field, language study, children's schooling, assistance to the national

church, equipment over area-specified amounts, financial requests to Boys and Girls Missionary Challenge (BGMC), Light for the Lost (LFTL), and Speed the Light (STL), and departure for furlough.

4. Financial concerns and how to understand the mission-produced financial statements and cash receipts statements.

5. Missionary life and work is examined. This will involve teaching on time management, organizational skills, aligning a missionary's vision with his goals and the reality of his work, a process of self-evaluation, and identifying a set of best practices for missionary life.

6. Focus on health and wellness attitudes and practices. This will include emotional, physical, social, intellectual, and spiritual wellness and wholeness.

7. Missionary life and cultural issues are examined to help missionaries adapt to cross-cultural life and work. This will help new missionaries understand what biculturalism, cultural relativity, and biblical absolutism means, identify specific areas where their host culture differs from their home culture, develop an understanding of how their new culture views time, face, patron-client relationships, education and competence orientations, flexibility and adjustment orientations, and interdependence orientations. This will also help the new missionary develop a strategy to deal with cultural adjustments and culture shock.

8. Missionary relationships are examined to help new missionaries achieve good relationships with their missionary and national peers. This involves identifying areas of interpersonal problems, understanding how to deal with conflict and developing an attitude of loving relationships within the missionary's family, other missionaries, and the national church.

Missionary Retreats for New and Veteran Missionaries

Retreats occur in each area within the Asia Pacific Region on differing time frames. However, each area attempts to have a retreat in a one to two year repeating cycle. The retreats are a time for veteran and new missionaries to mingle, share concerns and needs, and to develop relationships. They are also a time when the strategy to contribute to missionary longevity can develop.

Findings

The study found several items crucial to missionary longevity. These findings were implemented into the Asia Pacific Region's missionary training strategies as a direct result of this research.

1. Missionaries are dependent upon their relationship with God and reliance upon the protection of the Holy Spirit.

2. The missionary's sense of divine calling gives her or his vocation special significance and the ability to stay the course during hard times. A number of veterans responded to the survey in chapter seven citing the sense of call as a major factor in their continuing during the hardest times.

3. Relationships between missionaries and their peers, the national church, and mission leadership were important to missionary longevity and success.

4. Culture shock was another important factor in missionary attrition and the region implemented in its strategy a process of dealing with this in training sessions for new missionaries at mission headquarters and on the field.

Conclusion

Missionary attrition damages Asia Pacific's on-going effort to reach the world in the twenty-first century. The research in this study revealed that attrition in the Asia Pacific Region comes from a consistent set of reasons. Some of these reasons, such as retirement or death, were not addressed in this project. However, factors such as culture shock and issues involving the family, AGWM organizational structure, leadership, relationships with other missionaries and the national church can be intentionally addressed. This project, after identifying the issues, addressed the ones that affect missionary longevity through pre-field and on-field training. For new missionaries, the pre-field training occurred during the new missionary training sessions set aside for each region during AGWM's annual Missionary Renewal. In these meetings, the new missionaries were exposed to veteran missionaries who discussed cultural, relational, and family issues. These times were structured so that the new missionary interacts and asks questions of the veterans. New missionary training continued to on-field venues where they were exposed to field specific issues and cultural idiosyncrasies. These training sessions included veteran and field leaders who helped mentor the new missionaries.

On-going training for veteran missionaries was also included in this project. Veteran issues are similar to new missionary issues in that they involve relationship and family issues. These were dealt with in a conscious manner during the annual

Regional Studies sessions, which took place during AGWM's Missionary Renewal for veteran and new missionaries. Each missionary attends when he or she is conducting deputational ministry in the U.S.A. These sessions focused on elements that contribute to resiliency, which in turn contributes to missionaries overcoming depression and burnout. Veteran missionaries were also exposed to positive training during on-field missionary retreats in the various areas of the Asia Pacific Region. Missionary longevity is the goal of the Asia Pacific Region and this project improves the ability of the region to address issues that cause missionaries to fail.

This project has been personally meaningful for several reasons. It has allowed me as Asia Pacific Regional Director to research the history of Asia Pacific between the years of 1986 and 2005 to better understand the major reasons personnel left missions. Beyond the research, it has helped give greater focus toward ways to address attrition in positive, constructive settings. New material has been developed to assist personnel at the initial stage of their mission career. On-field training has also been expanded to help missionaries transition more easily after reaching their place of assignment. The Asia Pacific leadership team has had meaningful interaction in the past two years as we have discussed how best to help mission personnel finish well. We have worked together to develop material that addresses the need and I believe will help the Asia Pacific personnel in the future to have longer, more successful mission careers.

www.ingramcontent.com/pod-product-compliance
Lightning Source LLC
Chambersburg PA
CBHW060409090426
42734CB00011B/2270